Collected Sermons of Smith Wigglesworth
Volume I

Collected Sermons of Smith Wigglesworth
Volume I

©2011 Bottom of the Hill Publishing
All rights reserved. No part of this book may be used or reproduced in any manner without written permission except for brief quotations for review purposes only.

Printed in the United States of America and Australia.

Bottom of the Hill Publishing
Memphis, TN
www.BottomoftheHillPublishing.com

ISBN: 978-1-61203-326-6

Contents

Workers together with God	6
Preparation for the Second Coming	21
Immersed in the Holy Ghost	34
Active Life of the Spirit-filled Believer	36
The Way to Overcome: Believe	42
Our Calling, part 1	45
Our Calling, part 2	55
Ye are Our Epistle, part 1	68
Ye are Our Epistle, part 2	76
Great Grace Upon the Church	85
Greater Works Than These	90
Like Precious Faith, part 1	95
Like Precious Faith, part 2	99
The Power of Christ's Resurrection	104
What wilt Thou have Me to do?	107

Workers together with God

Preached in Angelus Temple, Bible Study #15 July 28, 1927

Interpretation of Tongues:
God has come to visit us and He has revealed Himself unto us, but He wants you to be so ready that nothing that He says will miss. He wants to build you on the foundation truth.

Are you ready this morning? What for? Because God has something better than yesterday. Higher ground, holier thoughts, more concentrated, clearer ministry God wants us every day to be in a rising tide. It is a changing of faith. It is an attitude of the spirit. It is where God rises higher and higher.

God wants us to come into the place where we will never look back. God has no room for the man that looks back, thinks back, or acts back.

The Holy Ghost wants to get you ready for stretching yourself out to God and believe that He is a rewarder of them that diligently seek Him. You need not use vain repetition. Ask and believe.

People come with their needs, they ask, they go away still with their needs because they do not faithfully wait to receive what God has promised them. If they ask they will get it.

Many people are missing the highest order. I went to a person who was full of the Spirit, but was all the time saying, "Glory! Glory! Glory!"

I said, "You are full of the Holy Ghost, but the Spirit cannot speak because you continually speak." He kept still then and the Spirit began speaking through him. We are altogether in the way of God. Do more believing and less begging.

I want so to change your operation in God till you will know that God is operating through you for this time and forevermore more. May the Spirit awake us to deep things today.

Are you ready? What for? That you may move and be moved by the mighty power of God that cannot be moved and so chastened and built up till you are in the place, it doesn't matter where the wind blows or difficulty comes, you are fixed in God.

Are you ready? What for? To come into the plan of the Most High God, believing what the Scripture says, and holding fast that which is good, believing so that no man shall take your crown.

The Word Changes the Believer
God can so change us by His Word that we are altogether different day by day David knew this. He said, "Thy word hath quickened me. He sent his word and healed me." How beautiful that God can make His Word abound! "I have hid thy word in my heart that I might not sin against thee."

It is absolutely infidelity and unbelief to pray about anything in the Word of God. The Word of God has not to be prayed about, the Word of God has to be received. If you will receive the Word of God, you will always be in a big place. If you pray about the Word of God the devil will be behind the whole thing. Never pray about anything which is "Thus saith the Lord." It has to be yours to build you on a new foundation of truth.

I want to turn your attention this morning to the sixth chapter of 2 Corinthians. This is a summit position for us, although there are many ground lines to be examined to see if we are rising to the summit of these glorious experiences. This is also ground work for deep heart searching. This is divine revelation of the spiritual character to us. The writer must have been immersed in this holy place.

If you turn to the first verse of Romans 12 you will see that the speaker is operated by an operation. He has been mightily under the operation on more than a surgical table. He has been cut to the very depths, till he has reached a place absolutely on the altar of full surrender. And out of the depths of it when he has got it there, now he is giving his whole life, as it were, in a nutshell.

I beseech you, therefore, brethren, by the mercies of God, that ye present your bodies a living sacrifice, holy, acceptable unto God, which is your reasonable service —Romans 12:1.

Here in this sixth chapter of 2 Corinthians we have again a beautiful word which ought to bring us to a very great place of hearing by the hearing of faith.

"We then, as workers together with him. . .

It is a collective thought. It is preaching to the whole Church in Christ Jesus. Paul has the Corinthians in his mind because the Corinthian church was the first church amongst the Gentiles, and he was the apostle to the Gentiles.

Receive Not God's Grace in Vain
"We then, as workers together with him, beseech you also that

ye receive not the grace of God in vain" (2 Corinthians 6:1). This is one of the mightiest words there is in the Scripture. People are getting blessed all the time, having revelation, and they go from one point to another but do not establish themselves in that thing which God has brought to them.

If you do not let your heart be examined when the Lord comes with blessing or correction, if you do not make it a stepping stone, if you do not make it a rising place, then you are receiving the grace of God in vain. People could be built far greater in the Lord and be more wonderfully established if they would move out sometimes and think over the graces of the Lord.

Grace is to be multiplied on conditions. How? In the first chapter of 2 Timothy we have these words: "the unfeigned faith that is in thee."

Everyone in this place, the whole Church of God, has the same like precious faith within him. And if you allow this like precious faith to be foremost, utmost on everything, you will find that grace and peace are multiplied.

Just the same the Lord comes to us with His mercy and if we do not see that the God of grace and mercy is opening to us the door of mercy and utterances, we are receiving it in vain.

I thank God for every meeting. I thank God for every blessing. I thank God every time a person says to me, "God bless you, Brother!" I say, "Thank you, Brother. The Lord bless you!" I see it is a very great place to have people desirous that we shall be blessed.

If we want strength in building in our spiritual character, we should never forget the blessings. When you are in prayer remember how near you are to the Lord. It is a time that God wants you to change strength there, and He wants you to remember He is with you.

When you open the sacred pages and the light comes right through and you say, "Oh, isn't that wonderful!" thank God, for it is the grace of God that has opened your understanding.

When you come to a meeting like this, the revelation comes forth, you feel this is what you wanted, receive it as the grace of the Lord. God has brought you to a place where He might make you a greater blessing.

Constant Salvation

For he saith, I have heard thee in a time accepted, and in the day of salvation have I succored thee: behold, now is the accepted time; behold, now is the day of salvation —2 Corinthians 6:2.

Two processes of salvation. He succored you when the Spirit was moving you and when the adversary was against you, when your neighbors and friends wished it not to be and when everybody rose up in accusation against you. When you know there were fightings without and fightings within, He succored you. He covered you till you came into salvation. And then He keeps you in the plan of His salvation.

This is the day of salvation. Being saved does not mean to say that you were not saved, but that you are being continually changed, in the process of regeneration being made like unto God, being brought into the operation of the Spirit's power, being made like unto Him.

This is the day of salvation. He has succored thee in a time when Satan would destroy thee, and He is with thee now.

This is the day of salvation. If we remain stationary, God has nothing for us. Everybody must see that they must be in progress. Yesterday will not do for today. I must thank God for yesterday Tomorrow is what I am today

Today: inspiration, divine intuition, where God is ravishing the heart, breaking forth all shorelines, getting my heart only responsive to His cry, where I live and move honoring and glorifying God in the Spirit. This is the day of visitation of the Lord. This is the great day of salvation, being moved on, into, for God.

Interpretation of Tongues:

It is the Lord. Let Him do what seemeth Him well. It may be death, but He has life in the midst of death.

We will praise and magnify the Lord, for He is worthy to be praised!

He has succored us, and now He is building us. Now He is changing us. Now we are in the operation of the Holy Ghost. You must every day make higher ground. You must deny yourself to get on with God. You must refuse everything that is not pure and holy and separate. God wants you pure in heart. He wants your intense desire after holiness.

"Seek ye first the kingdom of God, and his righteousness; and all these things shall be added unto you."

In Perfect Harmony

"Giving no offence in anything, that the ministry be not blamed" (2 Corinthians 6:3).

That is lovely! Oh! The church can be built. God will break down opposing things.

If you people in Angelus Temple are in a place where you would rather see one person saved here than two people saved at Bethel Temple, then you are altogether wrong and you need to be saved. If there is anybody here from Bethel Temple, if you would rather see one person saved in your temple than two people saved in Angelus Temple, then you are still out of order of the Spirit of the line of God and you are strangers to real holy life with God.

If your ministry is not to be blamed, how will it not be blamed? You have to live in love. See to it there is never anything comes out of your lips or by your acts that will interfere with the work of the Lord, but rather live in the place where you are helping everybody, lifting everybody, and causing everybody to come into perfect harmony For remember, there is always a blessing where there is harmony. "One accord" is the keynote of the victory that is going to come to us all the time.

There are thousands and thousands of different churches, but they are all one in the Spirit just in the measure as they receive the life of Christ. If there is any division, it is always outside the Spirit. The spiritual life in the believer never has known dissension or break, because where the Spirit has perfect liberty, then they all agree and there is no schism in the body

"The letter killeth, but the spirit giveth life." When there is division it is only because they take the letter instead of the Spirit. If we are in the Spirit, then we shall have life. If we are in the Spirit, we shall love everybody. If we are in the Spirit, there will be no division. There will be perfect harmony God wants to show us that we must so live in the Spirit that the ministry is not blamed.

It is a wonderful ministry God has given to us because it is a life ministry Pentecostal positions are spiritual positions. We recognize the Holy Ghost, but we recognize first the Spirit quickening us, saving us from every rudiment of evil power, transforming our human nature till it is in divine order. Then in that divine order we see that the Lord of Hosts can be very beautifully arranging the life till we live in the Spirit and are not fulfilling the lusts of flesh.

Interpretation of Tongues:

Let not thy goodness be evil spoken of, but so live in the spiritual life with Christ that He is being glorified over thy body, thy soul and thy spirit, till thy very life becomes emblematic and God reigns over thee in love and peace.

I like that because I see that when the Holy Ghost has perfect charge, He lifts and lightens and unveils the truth in a new way till we grip it.

Oh! What I would be if every one of us would go away this morning with this word in our heart, "Let not your goodness be evil spoken of." I know we all want to be good. It is not a wrong thing to desire that our goodness shall be appreciated. But we must watch ourselves because it is an evil day (although it is the day of salvation), and we must understand these days that the Lord wants to chasten and bring a people right into a full-tide position.

I believe that it is possible for God to sweep a company right into the glory before the Rapture just as well as at the Rapture. It is possible for you to be taken if others are left. May God grant unto us a very keen inward discerning of our heart's purity. We want to go. It is far better for us to go. But it is far better for the church that we stay.

If you comprehend the truth of this word which Paul realized was true, "It is far better for me to go," you will never take a pill nor use a plaster. You would never do anything to' save you from going if you believed it was better to go. There is a definite, inward motion of the power of God for the human life to so change it till we would not lift a finger, believing it was far better to go.

Then there is another side to it. Believing that God has us for the proclamation of the Gospel, for the building of the church, we would say, "Lord, for the purpose of being a blessing further for Thy sake, and for the sake of the Church, just keep us full of life to stay"

We would not be full of disease, but we would be full of life.

So the Lord grant unto us this morning a living faith to believe.

In Affliction for the Church

"But in all things approving ourselves as the ministers of God, in much patience, in afflictions, in necessities, in distresses" (2 Corinthians 6:4).

Now, these afflictions are not the afflictions of the disease class. Paul is very definite on these lines. He suffered afflictions with the people. Jesus suffered afflictions with the people. There can be many afflictions within our human frame on the line of feeling the association of our spiritual acquaintance is not ripening in the life of others.

You have to so live in the Spirit that when you see the church not rising into its glory, you have affliction for the church. You are sorry and deeply distressed because the church is not capturing the vision, and there is affliction in your sorrow.

God would have us so spiritual that we could have perfect discernment of the spirit of the people. If I can in a moment discern the spirit, whether it is quickening, whether the whole church is receiving it, whether my heart is moved by this power, then I can see the declination of positions, I can see the waning of positions, and I can see faith waning, and that will cause affliction and trouble to my life.

May God give us to realize that we are so joined to the Church that we may labor to bring the Church up. Paul said he travailed in birth for people to be formed again. It was not to be saved again. But they had missed apprehension. They had missed fellowship of divine order, so he labored again that they might be brought into this deep fellowship in the Spirit.

God help us to see that we can travail for the church. Blessed is the person who can weep between the door and the altar. Blessed is the people of God that can take Angelus Temple on their hearts and weep behind, cry through till the church is formed again, till she rises in glory till the power of heaven is over her, till the spiritual acquaintance rises higher and higher, till the song lifts them to the heights.

This is the order of the church of God. The ministry be not blamed, but a higher height, a glorious truth, a blessed fidelity, higher and higher.

"Possess Your Soul in Peace
In much patience."

There is a word which needs to be in these days. I know I am speaking to people who have churches and who have a lot to do in churches. Remember this: You never lose so much as when you lose your peace. If the people see that you have lost your groundwork of peace, they know you have got outside of the position of victory. You have to possess your soul in peace.

Strange things will happen in the church, things will look as though they were all contrary, and you will feel that the enemy is busy At that time possess your soul in peace. Let the people know that you have acquaintance with One Who, when He was reviled, reviled not again.

Let your patience be so possessed that you can suffer anything for the church or for your friends or for your neighbors, or anyone. Remember this: We build character in others as our character is built. Just as we are pure in our thought, tender and gracious to other people, and possess our souls in patience, then the people have great desire for our fellowship in the Holy Ghost.

Now Jesus was emblematic of that line. They saw Him undisturbed. I love to think about Him. He helps me so much because

He is the very essence of help.

Give Not Offense Nor Cause Distress
"In necessities and distresses." This means spiritual distresses because of acquaintance with the Church. It is the Church we are dealing with here. Paul is in a place where he is breathing forth by divine appointment to the Church.

The purpose of these meetings is to gather the Church together in fidelity lines, because if five people could save Sodom and Gomorrah, five holy people in a church can hold the power of the Spirit till Light shall reign. We do not want to seek to save ourselves, but lose ourselves that we may save the Church. You cannot help distresses coming. They will come, and offenses will come, but woe unto those that cause offenses. See that you do not cause offense. See that you live in a higher tide. See that your tongue cannot move.

I wonder if you have ever seen the picture in the twenty-second chapter of Luke, "Lord, is it I?" Every one of them was so conscious of his human weaknesses that not a single one of them had a place where he could say that it would not be he.

"One of you will betray me," Jesus said.

John was leaning on the breast of the Lord, and Peter beckoned to him and said, "Please get to know."' He knew if anybody could get to know it would be John.

How long do you think Jesus had known? He had known at least for nearly three years. He had been with them in the room, He had been feeding them, He had been walking up and down with them, and He had never told any of them it was Judas.

The church that follows Jesus should be so sober, sober to a sensitiveness that they would not speak against another, whether it was true or not.

Jesus is the great personality I have in every way to listen and also to be provoked by His holy inward generosity and purity, and also His acquaintance with love.

What would it have done? If He had told them, everyone would have been bitter against Judas. So He saved all His disciples from being bitter against Judas for three years.

What love! Can't you see that holy divine Savior? Every one of us today would throw ourselves at His feet. If we had a crown worth millions of money, we would say "You are worthy" O God, give us such a holy, intense, divine acquaintance that we would rather die than grieve Thee! Oh, for an inward savor that shall make us say

"A thousand deaths rather than sinning once." O Jesus, we worship Thee! Thou art worthy!

Interpretation of Tongues:

Into the very depths have I gone to succor thee. And in the very depths I called thee My own, and I delivered thee when thou wast oppressed and in oppression, and I brought thee out when thou wert sure to sink below the waves, and I lifted thee and brought thee into the banqueting house.

It is the mercy of the Lord. It is the love of the Lord. It is the grace of the Lord. It is the Spirit of the Lord. It is the will of the Lord.

Be ready Be alert for God. Live in the Holy Ghost. Oh, I can understand, "I would that ye all spake in tongues, but rather that ye prophesy except we have interpretation." I pray God that we may learn the lesson how to keep ourselves so that the Spirit shall blend, the harmony shall be beautiful. There is not a person in the place but is feeling the breath of the Almighty breathing over us. This is one of those moments when the Spirit is coming to us and saying, "Don't forget. This is the receiving of the grace of God." You are not to go away and forget. You are to go away and be what God intends you to be.

Apprehended in Sweden

"In stripes, in imprisonments, in tumults, in labours, in watchings, in fastings" (2 Corinthians 6:5). How those first apostles did suffer! And how we together with them do suffer.

Sweden is a most remarkable place in many ways. When I was in Sweden the power of God was upon me, and it was there that I was apprehended for preaching these wonderful truths, talking about the deep things of God, seeing people healed on every line.

The Lutheran churches, yes, and the doctors rose up like an army against me and had special meetings with the king to try to get me out of the country And at last they succeeded.' It was in Sweden that I was escorted out with two detectives and two policemen, because of the mighty powers of God moving amongst the people in Stockholm. But beloved, it was very lovely!

One of the nurses in the king's household came, and she was healed of a leg trouble — I forget whether a broken thigh or a dislocated joint. She went to the king and she said, "I have been so wonderfully healed by this man. You know I am walking all right now."

"Yes," he said, "I know everything about him. I know all about him. Tell him to go. I do not want him turned out. If he goes out, he can come back; but if he is turned out, he cannot come back."

I thank God I was not turned out, I was escorted out.

They went to see the policemen to see if I could have a big meeting in the park on the Whitsun Tide Monday. The policemen joined together and they said, "There is only one reason that we could refuse him, and it is on this line: if that man puts his hands upon the sick in the great park, it would take thirty more policemen to guard the situation. But if he will promise us that he will not lay his hands upon the people, then we will allow you to have the park."

They came and asked me, and I said, "Promise them. I know God is not subject to my laying hands upon the people. When the presence of the Lord is there to heal, it does not require hands. Faith is the great operation position. When we believe God all things are easy"

So they built places where I could speak to thousands of people.

I prayed, "Lord, You know. You have never been yet in any place fixed. You have ,the mind of all things. Show me how it can be done today without the people having hands laid upon them. Show me."

To the people I said, "All of you that would like the power of God going through you today, healing everything, put your hands up."

There was a great crowd of hands, thousands of hands went up. "Lord, show me."

And He told me as clearly as anything to pick a person out that stood upon a rock. It was a very rocky place. So I told them all to put their hands down but this person. To her I said, "Tell all the people what are your troubles."

She began to relate her troubles. From her head to her feet she was so in pain that she felt if she did not sit down or lie down she would never be able to go on.

"Lift your hands high," I said. Then, "In the name of Jesus I rebuke from your head to your feet the evil one, and I believe He has loosed you."

Oh, how she danced and how she jumped and how she shouted!

That was the first time that God revealed to me it could be done. We had hundreds healed without touching them and hundreds saved without touching. Our God is a God of mighty power. Oh, how wonderful, how glorious and how fascinating it is that we can come into a royal place! This is a royal place. We have a great God. We have a wonderful Jesus. I believe in the Holy Ghost.

In Prison in Switzerland

". . . in imprisonments."

In Switzerland I have been put into prison twice for this wonderful work. But praise God, I was brought out all right!

The officers said to me, "We find no fault. We are so pleased. We have found no fault because you are such a great blessing to us in Switzerland."

And in the middle of the night they said, "You can go."

I said, "No. I will only go on one condition. That is that every officer there is in the place gets down on his knees and I pray with all of you."

Glory to God!

A High Tide

Are you ready? What for? To believe the Scriptures. That is necessary. The Scripture is our foundation to build upon properly. Christ is the cornerstone. We are all in the building.

Oh! If I could let you see that wonderful city coming down out of heaven, millions, trillions beyond countless numbers, a city coming down out of heaven to be married, millions, trillions of people making the city.

Get ready for that. Claim your rights in God's order this morning. Do not give way. If you hear any spiritual breathing from anyone, believe that is your order. If you see Christ, believe He was your firstfruit. If you see Paul by the Holy Ghost penetrating your divine position, believe it is yours.

Have faith in God. Believe the Scripture is for you. If you want a high tide rising in the power of God, say, "Give me, Lord, that which I shall be short in nothing." Have a real faith. Believe that love covers you, His life flows through you, His quickening Spirit lifts you.

Prayer

O God, take these people into Thy great pavilion. Lead them, direct them, preserve them, strengthen them, uphold them by Thy mighty power. Let the peace that passeth understanding, the joy of the Lord, the comfort of the Holy Ghost be with them. Amen.

Questions and Answers

Q: In Ephesians 6:12 does "wrestling" mean wrestling in prayer? "For we wrestle not against flesh and blood, but against principalities," etc.

A: According to 2 Corinthians 10:5, we are able to smite the enemy and bring every thought into perfect obedience to the law of Christ.

"Casting down imaginations, and every high thing that exalteth itself against the knowledge of God, and bringing into captivity every thought to the obedience of Christ."

Now is that through prayer, or how? It is quite clear to me that faith inspires you to pray but faith will command you to command. And if you are in the place of real faith when these things come up against you, you will say "Get thee behind me" Luke 4:8 no matter what it is.

Prayer is without accomplishment unless it is accompanied by faith. Jude says we can pray in the Holy Ghost. Be sure you are filled with the Spirit that you do not pray but Another prays. Be sure you are filled with the life of Christ till faith rises, claims, destroys, brings down imagination and everything that opposes Christ. Faith and prayer, an act, a command.

Q: Which is the right way to baptize, in the name of Jesus, or the Father, Son, and Holy Ghost?

A: Always do that which causes no contention and no split. Water baptism in the name of Jesus causes more trouble than anything else, and you should never have trouble in the church, you should be at peace. The Lord said it was to be in the name of the Father, Son, and Holy Ghost, and when we keep in the right order, as He said, then there is no schism in the body.

When you go on your own line and strike out a new cord, you cause dissension and trouble. This thing has caused more trouble than anything because it has not been satisfied to go there. It has gone further and said that Jesus is the Father, Jesus is the Son, and Jesus is the Holy Ghost. If you do not keep on the right line, keep in the words where Jesus was, you will be toppled over in awful distress and darkness. Keep on the high line.

Q: What should be our attitude toward the coming of the Lord? Should we be enjoying His personal presence now, disregarding the time of His coming, or should we wait and anticipate His coming?

A: Do what Peter did. He hastened to the coming, and he left everything behind him to catch the gleam of it. You have to keep your mind upon it, looking unto and hastening it. It is a joy to the Church. It is that "blessed hope." It is that glorious appearing. And it will save you from any amount of things, for he that looks for that purifieth himself.

Q: Does a person have to go to school in order to save souls?

A: I think you will save more souls out of the school. What you have got to do is to understand that soul-saving work is never made in schools. Soul-saving work is the regenerative of the spirit, of the life, to make you eaten up with the zeal of the Lord. Soul saving is the best thing. It is the sure place, it is the right place, and I hope we are doing it when He comes.

Q: Is the Spirit of God within the individual that is born again? I have always thought so from the eighth chapter of Romans.

A: If you will rightly consider the truth and keep it before you, it will save you from any amount of error. The epistles are for people who are baptized in the Holy Ghost, baptized believers.

When you say, "Except you have the Spirit of Christ, you are none of His," Romans 8:9, you will find that is a perfect word right in the epistles. The new birth has within it the Spirit of Jesus, and it has the word also, "My word is spirit and life." It is not the Holy Spirit; it is the Spirit of Jesus.

The Holy Spirit is that which comes after, and is with you all the time. He was with you in revelation of conviction, but when you were filled He came inside. And after He comes inside, it is so much different from being outside.

Q: Did Jesus think it not robbery to be equal with God? What did He mean by saying that?

A: It meant He was equal in power, equal in authority, equal in the glory. He was perfectly one, and what His Father was, He was, perfectly joined. Yet in order for perfect obedience, that all the people should learn obedience, He left the glory left everything behind to save us. He had as much right to stop and say, "Father, You go," but He was willing to go and left the glory although He had the right to stop.

Q: If a contract were entered into by two people and broken by one party, should that be collected by law by the other party?

A: Yes, if you lived in the law. But if you lived in the Spirit, then you would not go to law with your brother. It depends upon whether you live in law or live in grace. If you live in grace, you will never go into law.

I thank God that I was in business for twenty-five years and might have picked up a lot of money, but it is still left there because I would not go to law. I do not believe in it.

But I am not a law to you people. I tell you what law is and I tell you what grace is.

Q: What is the seal put upon God's people?

A: The seal is the Holy Spirit. It is different from anything else. It is upon you, and the devil knows it. All the evil powers of the earth know it. You are sealed with that Holy Spirit of promise till the day of redemption. You are also baptized in the same Spirit, and that is in the epistles. But don't forget that you get a great deal in your salvation, in the new birth. Press on and get sealed with the Spirit.

All they which are in Christ will be caught up at His coming. The twenty-second chapter of Luke distinctly says that Jesus would not sit down again to break bread till the kingdom had come. Now the kingdom is in every believer, and He will not sit down till every believer is there. The kingdom is in the believer, and the kingdom will come and millions and millions of people, I am sure, will be there who never received the Holy Ghost. But they had the life of the Christ inside. When He comes Who is our life — it is not the Holy Ghost Who is the life; Christ is the life — when He comes Who is our life, then shall we go to the Life.

Q: Is it every Christian's privilege to have his eyes so preserved that he need never wear glasses?

A: One thing will take place with every person here. There are any number of people who have been praying ever since they were ten years old, and if praying and the life within them could have altered the situation, it would have been altered. But I see they are here today with gray hair, and white hair, meaning that the natural man decays and you cannot do what you like with it. But the supernatural man may so abound in the natural man that it never decays. It can be replaced by divine life.

There comes a time in life when at fifty or so all eyes, without exception, begin to be dim. But why? What kind of dimness? If we were living in the time of Moses we should not require glasses and we should have as good eyesight as he had. How do you know? Because those tables of stone that he carried were written on so that he could see or anybody else could see without glasses.

It doesn't mean to say that your eyes are any worse than were Moses'. It means to say that the natural man has had a change. I believe and affirm that the supernatural power can be so ministered to us that even our eyesight can be preserved right through. But I say this: Any person is a fool that professes to have faith and then gets a big printed Bible so that he will not need glasses. It presents a false position before the people. What he has got to see is if he will carry a Bible about in his hand which, as the whole of the Bible in very short space, his eyesight may require either some help or he may not be able to read correctly.

I have been preaching faith to our people for thirty years. When my daughter came back from Africa and saw her mother and myself with glasses, she was amazed. When our people saw us put glasses on the first time, they were very much troubled. They were no more troubled than we were. But I found it was far better to be honest with the people and acknowledge my place than get a Bible that was right big print and deceive the people and say that my eyesight was all right. I like to be true.

My eyesight gave way at about fifty-three, and somehow God is doing something. I am now sixty-eight, and I do not want any kind of glasses different, and I am satisfied God is restoring me.

When I was seeking this way of divine healing I was stumbled because all the people that had such testimony of divine healing were wearing glasses. I said, "I cannot go on with this thing. I am stumbled every time I see the people preaching divine healing wearing glasses." And I got such a bitterness in my spirit that God had to settle me on that line — and I believe yet that I have not fully paid the price.

My eyes will be restored, but until then I will not deceive anybody. I will use glasses till I can perfectly see.

A woman came up to me one day and I noticed she had no teeth.

"Why," I said, "your mouth is very uneven. Your gums have dropped in some places and the old gums are very uneven."

"Yes," she said, "I am trusting the Lord for a new set of teeth."

"That is very good," I said. "How long have you been trusting Him for them?"

"Three years."

"Look here," I said, "I would be like Gideon: I would put the fleece out and I would tell the Lord that I would trust Him to send me teeth in ten days or money to buy a set in ten days, and whichever came first I would believe it was He."

In eight days, fifty dollars came to her from a person whom she had never been acquainted with in any way, and it bought her a beautiful set of teeth — and she looked well in them.

A person is prayed for eyesight and as soon as he is prayed for, he believes, and God stimulates his faith, but his eyesight is about the same. "What shall I do?" he asks. "Shall I go away without my glasses?"

"Can you see perfectly?" I ask. "Do you require any help?"

"Yes. If I should go as I go now, I would stumble."

"Put your glasses on," I say. "For when your faith is perfected you will not require any glasses, and when God perfects your faith your glasses will drop off. But as long as you have need, use them."

You can take that for what you like, but I believe in common sense.

Preparation for the Second Coming of the Lord

Preached in Angelus Temple, Bible Study #21 August 11, 1927

I am conscious today that God has a design for us greater than our thoughts even or our language, and so I am not frightened of on the line of the spiritual exaggeration, shall I say. I dare believe that God will help me say things to you that shall inspire you to beginning dare to believe God.

Up to this present time the Lord's word is for us, "Hitherto ye have asked nothing." Surely you people that have been asking great things from God for a long time would be amazed if you entered into it with clear knowledge that it is the Master, it is Jesus, who has such knowledge .of the mightiness of the power of the Father, of the joint union with Him,, that nothing is impossible for you to ask. Surely it is He only Who could say "Hitherto you have asked nothing."

So God means me to press you another step forward. Begin to' believe on extravagant asking, believing that God is pleased when you ask large things.

If you will only dispose of yourself in a short time —for it is nothing but yourself that will hinder you — dispose of your human mind, dispose of your human measure, dispose of your strength and dispose of all you have — it is a big word for me to say — and let inspiration take whole charge of you, bring you out of yourself into the power of God, it may be today that God shall so transform you into another man as you have never been before.

Interpretation of Tongues:

Only the divine mind has divine thought to meet human order for knowing us from the beginning and understanding us as a Father and pitying us as children, He begins with the blade and the ear and the full corn in the ear so that we might know that He won't take us out of our death but He will transform us moment by moment till we can come into full stature of the mind and thought and prayer and act.

Hallelujah! God is on the throne.

Now beloved in the Lord, I come to you this morning to inspire you to dare believe that this day is for you as a beginning of days. You have never passed this way before. So I bring you to another day of passing over any heights, passing through mists or darkness, dare believe that the cloud is upon thee, shall break with an exceeding reward of blessing.

Don't be afraid of clouds. They are all earthly Never be afraid of an earthly thing. You belong to a higher order, a divine order, a spiritual order. Then believe that God wants you to soar high this morning.

Interpretation of Tongues:

Fear not to enter in, for the Lord thy God has thee now in preparation. He is proving thee and He is chastising thee, but His hand is not heavy upon thee as thou mayest think, for He is gentle and entreating to bring thee into the desired place of thy heart's affections.

Be still and know that I am God. It is I and I alone that openeth to thee the good treasure. Oh, to be still that my mind be so unsurfeited with the cares of this life that I might be able to enter into the joy and the bliss God has caused me to, for 1 have not passed this way hitherto.

So God is going to speak to us about entering into something we have not entered into before.

The thoughts of this morning message are primary to the message of the coming of the Lord. There must be a preparing place and an understanding line because of the purposes God is arranging for us. I know He is even at the door. Spiritual perception makes us know of His near return. But we must be so built on the line of truth that when He comes we are ready.

In the few days to come I am going to declare unto you the revelation of Christ to me of the readiness, and what it is, the knowledge of it, the power of it, the purpose of it, till every vestige of our human being is so filled with it, it would be impossible for us to be out of it. We shall be in the midst of it.

I have a message this morning leading up to the knowledge of His coming. It is in Peter's second epistle, the third chapter.

Knowing this first, that there shall come in the last days scoffers, walking after their own lusts, and saying, Where is the promise of his coming? for since the fathers fell asleep, all things continue as they were from the beginning of the creation. For this they willingly are ignorant of, that by the word of God the heavens were of old, and the earth standing out of the water and in the water: whereby the world that then was, being overflowed with water, perished: but the heavens and the earth, which are now, by the same word are kept in store, reserved unto fire against the day of judgment and perdition of ungodly men. But, beloved, be not ignorant of this one thing, that one day is with the Lord as a thousand years, and a thousand years as one day. The Lord is not slack concerning his promise, as some men count slackness; but is longsuffering to us-ward, not willing that any should perish, but that all should come to repentance. But the day of the Lord will come as a thief in the night; in which the heavens shall pass away with a great noise, and the elements shall melt with fervent heat, the earth also and the works that are therein shall be burned up. Seeing then that all these things shall be dissolved, what manner of persons ought ye to be in all holy conversation and godliness, Looking for and hasting unto the coming of the day of God, wherein the heavens being on fire shall be dissolved, and the elements shall melt with fervent heat? Nevertheless we, according to his promise, look for new heavens and a new earth, wherein dwelleth righteousness. Wherefore, beloved, seeing that ye look for such things, be diligent that ye may be found of him in peace, without spot, and blameless. And account that the longsuffering of our Lord is salvation —2 Peter 3:3-15.

I may deal with many things on the line of spiritual awakening, for this is what is needed this day. This day is a needy day of spiritual awakening, not so much as a knowledge of salvation but a knowledge of waking in salvation.

The seed of the Lord Jesus Christ is mightily in you, which is a seed of purifying, a seed of truth and knowledge, a seed of life-giving, a seed of transforming, a seed of building another person in the body till the body that bears the seed only lives to contain the body which the seed has made, until that comes forth with glorious light and power till the whole body has yielded itself to another, a fullness, a manifestation of the perfect formation of the Christ in you. This is the great hope of the future day.

I want to speak to you very exactly. All the people which are pressing into and getting ready for this glorious attained place where they shall not be found naked, where they shall be blameless, where they shall be immovable, where they shall be purified by the power of the Word of God, have within them a consciousness of the very presence of God within, changing their very nature and preparing them for a greater thing, and causing them to be ready for translation.

You will find that this thing is not now already in the world in perfection. There are millions and millions of real believers in Christ who are losing this great upward look, and in the measure they lose this upward look, they lose perfect purification. There is only perfect purification in this upward look.

When we see the day dawning, as the manifestation of the sons of God appear, just as these things come to us in light and revelation, we will find that it makes us know that everything is on the decay. Millions of people who are Christians believe this world is being purified. All the saints of God that get the real vision of this wonderful transformation of the body are seeing every day that the world is getting worse and worse and worse and ripening for judgment. And God is bringing us to a place where we which are spiritual are having, a clear vision that we must at any cost put off the works, of darkness. We must be getting ourselves ready for the glorious day.

These are last days. What will be the strongest confirmation for me to bring to you of the last days?

There are in the world two classes of believers. There are believers which are disobedient, or I ought to say there are children which are saved by the power of God which are disobedient children. And there are children which are just the same saved by the power of God who all the time are longing to be more obedient.

In this great fact Satan has a great part to play. It is on this factor in these last years that some of us have been brought to great grief at the first opening of the door with brazen fact to carnality forces. And we heard the word come rushing, through all over, "new theology" that damnable, devilish, evil power that lived in some of these disobedient children, which in these last days opened the door to the next thing.

As soon as this was noised abroad everywhere, "new theology," everybody began to say, "What is new theology?" Why, new theology is exactly on the same plane as being changed from monkeys to men. What does it mean? I want to make a clear sweep of that thing this morning. There is not a man can think on those lines only on atheism. Every person that touches a thing like that is an atheist behind all he has to say.

New theology was born in infidelity. It is atheism, and it opened the door for Russellism, which is full of false prophecy. Take the book of Russellism and go into, the prophecy. What was the prophecy? In 1924 the prophecy was that the Lord had to come. Russellism is false prophecy. Russellism is exactly the perfect plan of what will make the man of sin come forth. Russellism is preparing the door for the man of sin and they are receiving open-heartedly.

They declared that He would come in 1914. I went to see a dear beloved brother of mine who was so deluded by this false prophecy that he was utterly deceived by it. I said, "You will be deceived as sure as you live."

They said, "We are so sure it is true that if we are deceived we will give up all Russellism and have nothing to do with it."

But what does false prophecy do? False prophecy always makes a way out. The moment it did not come to pass they said they were mistaken in dates. What is the devil? If it had been a true prophecy He would have come. And the Word of God says if any prophecy does not come true that prophet has to prophesy no more.

But those people were deluded by the spirit of 'this world and the devil, which is the spirit of this world, and instantly allowed themselves to be gripped again, and the same prophet came forth saying that He was going to come in 1925.

In order to cover that, what did they do? They placarded in every nation, almost, in big cities, "Millions alive that will never, die." And they have been going at that now since 1925, and they are dying all the time, and their prophecy is still a cursed, evil prophecy. Still they go on.

The spirit of this age is to get you to believe a lie. If you believe a lie, you cannot believe the truth When once you are seasoned with a lie against the Word of God, He sends you strong delusion that you shall believe a lie Who does? God does God is gracious over His Word His Word is from everlasting His Word is true.

When we see those things which are coming to pass, what do we know? We know the time is at hand. The fig tree is budding for these false prophecies and these positions

Now you see, they never stop at that They go on to say Christ never has risen. Of course, if ever you believe a lie, if ever you turn the Word of God to some other place, you cannot believe the truth after that.

Then the last days opened the door for that false demon power which is in the world rampant everywhere, putting up the most marvelous buildings — Christian Science, which is devilish, hellish, and deceivable. I am preaching to you this morning that you shall deliver yourself from this present-day evil thing. How shall you do it? You can do it only on one line. Let the seed in. Let the seed of truth, the seed of righteousness, this power of God, this inward incorruptible.

The seed of Christ is an inward incorruptible. The new birth, the new life, is a quickening power, incorruptible, dealing with corruptible, carnal things, evil, sensuous, devilish. And when it comes to the Word of God, the seed of the Word of God is the life of the Word and you are living the life of the Word of God and are tremendously transformed all the time by the Word of the Lord.

This is the last days. You go out in the world and there is no difficulty What are you going to do now? Is this a fact? Is this true? Aren't people today almost afraid of sending their sons to the colleges because they come out more devils than they went in? Isn't atheism right in the seat of almost all these colleges? Then what have you to do? How shall you possess your soul in peace? How shall you preserve your children? How shall you help them? You say they have to go because you want them to come out with certain letters to their names. You want them to progress in knowledge, but how shall you save your children?

Nothing but the Word can save them.

I wish all the young men in this place would read these words 'in the first epistle of John: "Young men,.. .ye are strong,. . .and. . .have overcome the wicked one" (1 John 2:14). What by? By the Word.

They are mighty words we read in this Scripture. What does it say? The Word is holding these things, even the fires that are going to burn the world. The Word is holding them. What is the Word? The Word is the mighty power of the revelation to us of the Son of God. And the Son of God is holding all these powers today in the world, ready for the greatest conflagration that ever could be, when the heavens shall be burnt up, when the earth shall melt with fervent heat.

The Word of God is keeping these things reserved, all ready. What manner of men ought we to be in all manner of conversation in purifying ourselves.

Remember this: In heaven the glory, the revelation, the power, the presence, that which makes all heaven so full of beauty, is that time has no count. It is so lovely! A thousand years are as a day and a day as a thousand years.

Interpretation of tongues:

All the springs are in thee, all the revelations are in the midst of thee. It is He, the mighty God! It is He, the King of kings! It is He, the Son of the living God who is in the very innermost being of thy human nature, making thee know that before these things shall come to pass thou shalt be preserved in the midst of the flame. Whatever happens, God shall cover thee with His mighty covering;

and that which is in thee is incorruptible and undefiled and fadeth not away, which is reserved in the glory.

God says to us, "In patience possess thy soul." How beautiful! Oh! How the enrichment of the presence of the power of the Most High is bursting forth upon our — what shall I say? — our human frame. Something greater than the human frame.

Knowest thou not that that which is born to thee is greater than anything formed around thee? Knowest thou not that He which has been begotten in thee, is the very God of power to preserve thee, and to bring forth light and truth and cause the vision to be made clearer?

You notice this: There is an elect of God. I know that God has in this place people who, if you would examine yourself, you would be amazed to find that you are elect of God.

People are tremendously afraid of this position because they have heard so much on this line: "Oh, you know you are the elect of God! You are sure to be all right." There have been in England great churches which were laid out upon these things. I thank God that they are all withered. You will find if you go to England those strong people that used to hold all these things are almost withered out. Why? Because they went on to say whatever you did, if you were elect, you were right. That is wrong.

The elect of God are those that are pressing forward. The elect of God cannot hold still. They are always on the wing. Every person that has a knowledge of the elect of God realizes it is important that he press forward. He cannot endure sin nor darknesses nor shady things. The elect is so in earnest to be elect for God that he burns every bridge behind him.

"Knowing this, that first there shall be a falling away"

Knowing this, that first God shall bring into His treasury the realities of the truth and put them side by side — the false, the true, those that can be shaken in mind, and those that cannot be shaken. God wants us to be so built upon the foundation of truth that we cannot be shaken in our mind, it doesn't matter what comes.

When I was in Sydney they said, "Whatever you do, you must see this place that they built for the man, the new man coming."

Theosophy has a new man. Nothing but theosophy could have a new man. The foundation of the theosophy has always been corruptible. From the beginning it has been corruptible. In the formation of theosophy it was joined up to Bradlaw one of the greatest atheists of the day. So you can only expect theosophy to be atheism. It sprung out of atheism.

The "Man of Sin" as 'he comes forth will do many things. There will be many false Christs and they will be manifestations of the forthcoming of the Man of Sin, but they will all come to an end. There will be the Man of Sin made, manifest.

These people are determined to have a man. They know someone has to come. We know Who He is that is coming. They begin to make a man. So they find a man in India, they polish him up as much as they can, and they make him as — well, in appearance, but you know we are told by the Lord that there is soft clothing goes onto wolves' backs.

We find they are going 'to bring this man forth in great style. When I went around the amphitheater in Sydney that was made for this man to come, I saw as clearly as anything it was the preparation for the Man of Sin. But they do not believe that.

What will make you to know it is the Man of Sin? This: Every religious sect and creed there is in the world all joins to it. Romanism you see joined up with it. Buddhism joined with it. There is not a religion known but what is joined up to it.

Why that is exactly what the devil will have. He will have all the false religions joining right up and the Man of Sin, when he comes, will be received with great applause

Who will be saved? Who will know the day? Who knows now the Man of Sin? Why, we feel when we touch him, when he opens his mouth, when he writes through the paper, when we see his actions — we know who he is.

What has the Man of Sin always said? Why, exactly what Russellism says What? No hell The devil has always said that What does Christian Science say? No hell, no devil They are ready for him. The devil has always said no hell, no evil. And these people are preparing, and they do not know it, for the Man of Sin.

We have to see that these days have to come before the Lord can come. There has to be ,a falling away. There has to be a manifestation in this day so clear, of such undeniable fact. I tell you, when they begin to build temples for the Man of Sin to come (but they don't know it), you know the day is at hand.

A person said to me, "You see, the Christian Scientists must be right — look at the beautiful buildings. Look at all the people following them."

Yes, everybody can belong to it. You can go to any brother you like, you can go to any theater you like, you can go to any race course you like, you can be mixed up with the rest of the people in your life and still be a Christian Scientist. You can have the devil right and left and anywhere, and still belong to Christian Science.

When the Man of Sin is come, he will be hailed 'on all sides. When he is manifested, who will miss him? Why the reverent, the holy the separated. How will they miss him? Because they will not be here to greet him!

But there will be things that will happen prior to his coming that we shall know. You can tell. I am like one this morning that is moving with a liquid, holy, indispensable, real fire in my bosom, and I know it is burning and the body is not consumed. It is real fire from heaven that is making my utterances come to you to know that He is coming. He is on the way God is going to help me tell you why you will know. You that have the breath of the Spirit, there is something now moving as I speak As I speak, this breath of mighty, quickening, moving, changing, desirable power is making you know and it is this alone that is making you know that you will be ready.

No matter who misses it, you will be ready. It is this I want to press upon you this morning, that you will be ready. And you won't question your position. You will know. Ah! Thank God, ye are not of the night. Ye are of the day. It shall not overtake you as a thief. Ye are the children of day. You are not the night. You are not drunken. Yes, you are. There is so much intoxication from this holy incarnation that makes you feel all the time you have to have Him hold you up. Praise the Lord! Holy intoxication, inspired revelation, invocation, incessantly inwardly moving your very nature, that you know as sure as anything that you do not belong to those who are putting off the day. You are hastening unto the day you are longing for the day.

You say "What a great day!" Why do you say it? Because the creature — Is this body the creature? No. This is the temple that holds the creature. The creature inside the temple longeth, travaileth, groaneth to be delivered, and will be delivered. It is the living creature. It is the new creature. It' is the new creation. It is the new nature. It is the new life.

What manner of men ought we to be? I am going to read it:

The Lord is not slack concerning his promise, as some men count slackness; but is longsuffering to us-ward, not willing that any should perish, but that all should come to repentance —2 Peter 3:9.

I want you to notice this: This is not the wicked repentant. The epistles are always speaking to the saints of God. When I speak to you saints of God, you will, find that my language will make you see that there is not within you one thing that has to be covered. I say it without fear of contradiction, because it is my whole life, inspired by the truth. You know that these meetings will purify you.

It is on this line that every time you hear people speak upon this — I do not mean as a theory. This is not a theory There is a difference between a man standing before you on theory He has chapter and verse, line upon line, precept upon precept, and he works it. out upon the scriptural basis. It is wonderful, it is good, it is inspiring; but I am not there this morning. Mine is another touch. Mine is the spiritual nature showing to you that the world is ripening for judgment. Mine is a spiritual acquaintance bringing you to a place of separation, holiness unto God, that you may purify yourself and be clean, ready for the great day.

This is the day of purifying. This is the day of holiness. This is the day of separation. This is the day of waking. O God, let us wake today! Let the inner spirit wake into consciousness that God is calling us. The Lord is upon us. We see that the day is upon us. We look at the left side, we look at the right side, we see everywhere new theories. New things will not stand the light of the truth When you see these, things, you know that there must be a great falling away before the day And it is coming. It is upon us.

Paul said he travailed in birth. Jesus did the same. John had the same. So brothers and sisters, may God bless you and make you see that this is a day of travailing for the Church of God that she might be formed so that she is ready for putting on the glorious raiment of heaven forever and forever.

Seeing then that all these things shall be dissolved, what manner of persons ought ye to be in all holy conversation and godliness, Looking for and hasting unto the coming of the day of God, wherein the heavens being on fire shall be dissolved, and the elements shall melt with fervent heat?

Nevertheless we, according to his promise, look for new heavens and a new earth, wherein dwelleth righteousness. Wherefore, beloved, seeing that ye look for such things, be diligent that ye may be found of him in peace, without spot, and blameless —2 Peter 3:11-14.

Without spot! WITHOUT SPOT! Without spot and blameless!

Do you believe it? Who can do it? THE BLOOD CAN DO IT! The blood, the blood, oh the blood! The blood of the Lamb! The blood of Jesus can do it. Spotless, clean, preserved for God.

Give the devil the biggest chase of his life and say these words, "The blood of Jesus Christ, God's Son, cleanseth us from all unrighteousness."

If ever you hear a row like that in any Christian Science meeting about the blood of Jesus, go and I will tell you they are being converted. If you ever hear, tell of Russellism getting excited over the blood of Jesus, I can tell you God has dealt with them. If ever you hear about this new man in theosophy getting excited about the blood of Jesus, you can tell them from Wigglesworth that there is a new order in the world. But they have no room for the blood. And yet we see the blood is preparing us for this great day.

In the amphitheater in Sydney, when I spoke about the blood and when I spoke about this infernal thing, the whole place was upset. You be careful when anybody comes to you with a sugar-coated pill or with a slimy tongue. They are always of the devil. The Spirit of the Lord will always deal with truth. These people never deal with truth. They always cover up the truth. "Oh, you know, we are all sons of God. We all belong to God." That is what people said when Jesus was here, and He said, "You are mistaken. You belong to the devil." And if Jesus dared say things like that, I dare.

Questions and Answers

Q: Is it true if we believe a lie we cannot believe the truth?

A: That is not what I said. If you once believe the Word of God to be a lie, then you cannot believe the truth of the Word of God. The Word of God comes to you like life and revelation, but' Satan in his spurious condition comes, as he has done with many and moved them from truth to believe in some theory of truth. They have gotten a theory of something else which is not truth and they have denied the truth to take hold of the theory It is all theory when people have left the truth. The people that live in truth never have a theory; it is always fact.

Q: Because I have laid aside my Christian Science books, the people are now using what they call "malicious magnetism" against me. I know Jesus is stronger than they.

A: This is a very important thing. There are many people so under delusion and devil oppressed on these lines that they join together to damage the character of others because they do not go their way. That is the devil if nothing else is. The greatest fact about Christian Science's false position is that they are led captive by the father of liars. He has been a liar from the beginning. They have stepped out of truth and been taken in charge by this monster devil till they cannot believe the truth.

"I am 'the light of the world'; any man that walketh in me shall not be in darkness. I am the light to light every man that cometh into the world."

If you will go back to the time when you knew the light of the truth was burning through you, you will find that there you turned from that to take something else which was not light. Keep in the light and there is no power of Satan. If a hundred people came and stood around you and said to you, "We will join together to bind you that you shall be crippled," or your mind he affected, or anything, if you know you have the Light you can smile and say, "You can do nothing to me."

Never be afraid of anything There are two things in the world one is fear, the other faith. One belongs to the devil; the other to God. If you believe in God, there is no fear. If you sway toward any delusion of Satan, you will be brought into fear. Fear always brings bondage. There is a place of perfect love to Christ where you are always casting out all fear and you are living in the place of freedom.

Be sure that you never allow anything to make you afraid. God is for you, who can be against you?

The secret of many people going into Christian Science is a barren church that had not the Holy Ghost. Christian Science exists because the churches have a barren place because they haven't the Holy Ghost. There would be no room for Christian Science if the churches were filled with the Holy Ghost. But because the churches had nothing, then the needy people went to the devil and he persuaded them they had something, and they are coming out knowing they have got nothing only a wilderness experience.

Let us save ourselves from all this trouble by letting the Holy Ghost fill our hearts.

> Will you be baptized in this faith,
> Baptized in the Holy Ghost?
> To be free indeed 'tis the power you need,
> Baptized in the Holy Ghost.

Don't depend on any past tense, any past momentum, but let the unction be upon you, let the presence and the power be upon you. Are you thirsty? Longing? Desiring? Then God will pour out of His treasures all you need. God wants to satisfy us with His great, abounding, holy love, imparting love upon love and faith upon faith.

The secret of all declension is refusal of the Holy Ghost. If you have fallen short, it is because you refused the Holy Ghost. Let the Holy Ghost be light in you to lighten the light which is in you, and no darkness shall befall you. You will be kept in the middle of the road.

Hasten unto the coming of the Lord. Set your house in order. Be at peace. Live at peace. Forgive and learn how to forgive.

Never bear malice. Don't hold anybody any grudge. Forgive everybody It does not matter whether they forgive you or not, you forgive them. Live in forgiveness. Live in repentance. Live wholeheartedly. Set your house in order, for God's Son is coming to take that which is in the house.

Immersed in the Holy Ghost

The baptism of the Holy Ghost is a great beginning. I think the best word we can say is, "Lord, what wilt Thou have me to do?" The greatest difficulty today with us is to be held in the place where it shall be God only. It is so easy to get our own mind to work. The working of the Holy Ghost is so different. I believe there is a mind of Christ, and we may be so immersed in the Spirit that we are all the day asking, "What wilt Thou have me to do?"

This has been a day in the Holy Ghost. The last three months have been the greatest days of my life. I used to think if I could see such and such things worked I should be satisfied; but I have seen greater things than I ever expected to see, and I am more hungry to see greater things yet. The great thing at conventions is to get us so immersed in God that we may see signs and wonders in the name of the Lord Jesus; a place where death has taken place and we are not, for God has taken us. If God has taken hold of us we will be changed by His power and might. You can depend on it, the Ethiopian will be changed. I find God has a plan to turn the world upside down, where we are not.

When I have been at my wit's end, and have seen God open the door, I have felt I should never doubt God again. I have been taken to another place that was worse still. There is no place for us, and yet a place where God is, where the Holy Ghost is just showing forth and displaying His graces; a place where we will never come out, where we are always immersed in the Spirit, the glory of God being seen upon us. It is wonderful! There is a power behind the scenes that moves things. God can work in such a marvelous way....

I believe we have yet to learn what it would be with a Pentecostal Church in England that understood truly the work of intercession. I believe God the Holy Ghost wants to teach us that it is not only the people on the platform who can move things by prayer. You people, the Lord can move things through you. We have to learn the power of the breath of the Holy Ghost. If I am filled with the Holy Ghost, He will formulate the word that will come into my heart. The sound of my voice is only by the breath that goes through it. When I was in a little room at Bern waiting for my passport, I found a lot of people, but I couldn't speak to them. So I got hold of three men and pulled them unto me. They stared, but I got them on their knees. Then we prayed, and the revival began. I couldn't talk to them, but I could show them the way to talk to Someone else.

God will move upon the people to make them see the glory of God just as it was when Jesus walked in this world, and I believe the Holy Ghost will do special wonders and miracles in these last days. I was taken to see a young woman who was very ill. The young man who showed me the way said, "I am afraid we shall not be able to do much here, because of her mother, and the doctors are coming." I said, "This is what God has brought me here for," and when I prayed the young woman was instantly healed by the power of God. God the Holy Ghost says in our hearts today that it is only He who can do it. After that we got crowds, and I ministered to the sick among them for two hours.

The secret for the future is living and moving in the power of the Holy Ghost. One thing I rejoice in is that there need not be an hour or a moment when I do not know the Holy Ghost is upon me. Oh, this glorious life in God is beyond expression; it is God manifest in the flesh. Oh, this glorious unction of the Holy Ghost — that we move by the Spirit. He should be our continual life. The Holy Ghost has the last thoughts of anything that God wants to give. Glory to God for the Holy Ghost! We must see that we live in the place where we say, "What wilt Thou have me to do?" and are in the place where He can work in us to will and to do of His good pleasure.

The Active Life of the Spirit-filled Believer

Ministration and operation of the gifts

These are the last days; the days of the falling away. These are days when Satan is having a great deal of power. But we must keep in mind that Satan has no power only as he is allowed.

It is a great thing to know that God is loosing you from the world, loosing you from a thousand things. You must seek to have the mind of God on all things. If you don't, you will stop His working. I had to learn that as I was on the water en route to Australia. We stopped at a place called Aden, where they were selling all kinds of ware. Among other things were some beautiful rugs and ostrich feathers in great quantities. There was a gentleman in "first class" who wanted feathers. He bought one lot and the next lot put up was too big; he did not want so many. He said to me, "Will you join me?" I knew I did not want feathers for I had no room or use for them and wouldn't know what to do with them if I got them. However, he pleaded with me to join him. I perceived it was the Spirit as clearly as anything and I said, "Yes, I will." So the feathers were knocked down for fifteen dollars. Then I found the man had no money on him. He had plenty in his cabin. I perceived it was the Spirit again, so it fell to my lot to pay for the feathers. He said to me, "I will get the money and give it to one of the stewards." I replied: "No, that is not business. I am known all over the ship. You seek me out."

The man came and brought the money. I said, "God wants me to talk to you. Now sit down." So he sat down and in ten minutes' time the whole of his life was unhinged, unraveled, broken up, so broken that like a big baby he wept and cried for salvation. It was "feathers" that did it. But you know we shall never know the mind of God till we learn to know the voice of God. The striking thing about Moses is that it took him forty years to learn human wisdom, forty years to know his helplessness, and forty years to live in the power of God. One hundred and twenty years it took to teach that man, and sometimes it seems to me it will take many years to bring us just where we can tell the voice of God, the leadings of God, and all His will concerning us.

I see that all revelation, all illumination, everything that God had in Christ was to be brought forth into perfect light that we might be able to live the same, produce the same, and be in every activity sons of God with power. It must be so. We must not limit the Holy One. And we must clearly see that God brought us forth to make us supernatural, that we might be changed all the time on the line of the supernatural, that we may every day live so in the Spirit, that all of the revelations of God are just like a canvas thrown before our eyes, on which we see clearly step by step all the divine will of God.

Any assembly that puts its hand upon the working of the Spirit will surely dry up. The assembly must be as free in the Spirit as possible, and you must allow a certain amount of extravagance when people are getting through to God. Unless we are very wise, we can easily interfere and quench the power of God which is upon us. It is an evident fact that one man in a meeting, filled with unbelief, can make a place for the devil to have a seat. And it is very true, that if we are not careful we may quench the Spirit of some person who is innocent but incapable of helping himself. "We then that are strong ought to bear the infirmities of the weak." (Romans 15:1). If you want an assembly full of life you must have one in which the Spirit of God is manifested. And in order to keep at the boiling pitch of that blessed incarnation of the Spirit, you must be as simple as babies; you must be as harmless as doves and as wise as serpents (Matthew 10:16).

I always ask God for a leading of grace. It takes grace to be in a meeting because it is so easy if you are not careful, to get on the natural side. The man who is a preacher, if he has lost the unction, will be well repaid if he will repent and get right with God and get the unction back. It never pays us to be less than always spiritual, and we must have a divine language and the language must be of God. Beloved, if you come into real perfect line with the grace of God, one thing will certainly take place in your life. You will change from that old position of the world's line where you were judging everybody, and where you were not trusting anyone, and come into a place where you will have a heart that will believe all things; a heart that under no circumstances reviles again when you are reviled.

I know many of you think many times before you speak once. Here is a great word: "For your obedience is come abroad unto all men. I am glad therefore on your behalf: but yet I would have you wise unto that which is good, and simple concerning evil" (Romans 16:19). Innocent. No inward corruption or defilement, that is full of distrusts, but just a holy, divine likeness of Jesus that dares believe that God Almighty will surely watch over all. Hallelujah! "There shall no evil befall thee, neither shall any plague come nigh thy dwelling. For He shall give his angels charge over thee, to keep thee in all thy ways" (Psalm 91:10,11). The child of God who is rocked in the bosom of the Father has the sweetest touch of heaven, and the honey of the Word is always in it.

If the saints only knew how precious they are in the sight of God they would scarcely be able to sleep for thinking of His watchful, loving care. Oh, He is a precious Jesus! He is a lovely Savior! He is divine in all His attitude toward us, and makes our hearts to burn. There is nothing like it. "Oh," they said on the road to Emmaus, "did not our heart burn within us, as He walked with us and talked with us?" (Luke 24:32). Oh beloved, it must be so today.

Always keep in your mind the fact that the Holy Ghost must bring manifestation. We must understand that the Holy Ghost is breath, the Holy Ghost is Person, and it is the most marvelous thing to me to know that this Holy Ghost power can be in every part of your body. You can feel it from the crown of your head to the soles of your feet. Oh, it is lovely to be burning all over with the Holy Ghost! And when that takes place there is nothing but the operation of the tongue that must give forth the glory and the praise.

You must be in the place of magnifying the Lord. The Holy Ghost is the great Magnifier of Jesus, the great Illuminator of Jesus. And so after the Holy Ghost comes in, it is impossible to keep your tongue still. Why, you would burst if you didn't give Him utterance. Talk about a dumb baptized soul? Such a person is not to be found in the Scriptures. You will find that when you speak unto God in the new tongue He gives you, you enter into a close communion with Him hitherto never experienced. Talk about preaching! I would like to know how it will be possible for all the people filled with the Holy Ghost to stop preaching. Even the sons and daughters must prophesy. After the Holy Ghost comes in, a man is in a new order in God. And you will find it so real that you will want to sing, talk, laugh, and shout. We are in a strange place when the Holy Ghost comes in.

If the incoming of the Spirit is lovely, what must be the onflow? The incoming is only to be an onflow. I am very interested in scenery. When I was in Switzerland I wouldn't be satisfied till I went to the top of the mountain, though I like the valleys also. On the summit of the mountain the sun beats on the snow and sends the water trickling down the mountains right through to the meadows. Go there and see if you can stop it. Just so in the spiritual. God begins with the divine flow of His eternal power which is the Holy Ghost, and you cannot stop it.

We must always clearly see that the baptism with the Spirit must make us ministering spirits.

Peter and John had been baptized only a short time. Did they know what they had? No, I defy you to know what you have. No one knows what he has in the baptism with the Holy Ghost. You have no conception of it. You cannot measure it by an human standards. It is greater than any man has any idea of, and consequently those two disciples had no idea what they had. For the first time after they were baptized in the Holy Ghost they came down to the Gate Beautiful. There they saw the man sitting who for forty years had been lame. What was the first thing after they saw him? Ministration. What was the second? Operation. What was the third? Manifestation, of course. It could not be otherwise. You will always find that this order in the Scripture will be carried out in everybody.

I clearly see that we ought to have spiritual giants in the earth, mighty in apprehension, amazing in activity, always having a wonderful report because of their activity in faith. I find instead that there are many people who perhaps have better discernment than you, better knowledge of the Word than you, but they have failed to put it into practice, so these gifts lie dormant. I am here to help you to begin on the sea of life with mighty acts in the power of God through the gifts of the Spirit. You will find that this which I am speaking on is out of knowledge derived from a wonderful experience in many lands. The man who is filled with the Holy Ghost is always acting. You read the first verse of the Acts of the Apostles, "Jesus began both to do and teach." He began to do first, and so must we.

OUTWARD MANIFESTATION

Beloved, we must see that the baptism with the Holy Ghost is an activity with an outward manifestation. When I was in Norway, God was mightily moving there, though I had to talk by interpretation. However, God always worked in a wonderful way. One day we met a man who stopped the three men I was with, one being the interpreter. I was walking on, but I saw he was in a dilemma, so I turned back and said to the interpreter, "What is the trouble?"

"This man," he said, "is so full of neuralgia that he is almost blind and he is in a terrible state." As soon as ever they finished the conversation I said to the spirit that was afflicting him, "Come out of him in the name of Jesus." And the man said, "It is all gone! It is all gone! I am free." Ah, brothers, we have no conception of what God has for us!

I will tell you what happened in Sydney, Australia. A man with a stick passed a friend and me. He had to get down and then twist over, and the tortures on his face made a deep impression on my soul. I asked myself, "Is it right to pass this man?" So I said to my friend, "There is a man in awful distress, and I cannot go further. I must speak to him." I went over to this man and said to him, "You seem to be in great trouble." "Yes," he said, "I am no good and never will be." I said, "You see that hotel. Be in front of that door in five minutes and I will pray for you, and you shall be as straight as any man in this place." This is on the line of activity in the faith of Jesus. I came back after paying a bill, and he was there. I will never forget him wondering if he was going to be trapped, or what was up that a man should stop him in the street and tell him he should be made straight. I had said it, so it must be. If you say anything you must stand with God to make it so. Never say anything for bravado, without you have the right to say it. Always be sure of your ground, and that you are honoring God. If there is anything about it to make you anything, it will bring you sorrow. Your whole ministry will have to be on the line of grace and blessing. We helped him up the two steps, passed him through to the elevator, and took him upstairs. It seemed difficult to get him from the elevator to my bedroom, as though Satan was making the last stroke for his life, but we got him there. Then in five minutes' time this man walked out of that bedroom as straight as any man in this place. He walked perfectly and declared he hadn't a pain in his body.

Oh, brother, it is ministration, it is operation, it is manifestation! Those are three of the leading principles of the baptism with the Holy Ghost. And we must see to it that God is producing these three through us.

The Bible is the Word of God, it has the truths and whatever people may say of them they stand stationary, unmovable. Not one jot or tittle shall fail of all His good promises. His word will come forth. In heaven it is settled, on earth it must be made manifest that He is the God of everlasting power.

God wants manifestation and He wants His glory to be seen. He wants us all to be filled with that line of thought that He can look upon us and delight in us subduing the world unto Him. And so you are going to miss a great deal if you don't begin to act. But once you begin to act in the order of God, you will find that God establishes your faith and from that day starts you on the line of the promises. When will you begin?

WHAT IF WE BELIEVED?

In a place in England I was dealing on the lines of faith and what would take place if we believed God. Many things happened. But when I got away it appeared one man who worked in the colliery had heard me. He was in trouble with a stiff knee. He said to his wife, "I cannot help but think every day that that message of Wigglesworth's was to stir us to do something. I cannot get away from it. All the men in the pit know how I walk with a stiff knee, and you know how you have wrapped it around with yards of flannel. Well, I am going to act. You have to be the congregation." He got his wife in front of him. "I am going to act and do just as Wigglesworth did." He got hold of his leg unmercifully, saying, "Come out, you devils, come out! In the name of Jesus. Now, Jesus, help me. Come out, you devils, come out." Then he said, "Wife they are gone! Wife, they are gone. This is too good. I am going to act now." So he went to his place of worship and all the collier boys were there. It was a prayer meeting. As he told them this story these men became delighted. They said, "Jack, come over here and help me." And Jack went. As soon a he was through in one home he was invited to another, loosing these people of the pains they had gotten in the colliery.

Ah, brothers and sisters, we have no idea what God has for us if we will only begin! But oh, the grace we need! We may make a mishap. If you do it outside of Him, if you do it for yourself, and if you want to be someone, it will be a failure. We shall only be able to do well as we do it in the name of Jesus. Oh, the love that God's Son can put into us if we are only humble enough, weak enough, and helpless enough to know that except He does it, it will not be done! "What things soever ye desire when ye pray, believe that ye receive and ye shall have them."

Live in the Spirit, walk in the Spirit, walk in communion with the Spirit, talk with God. All leadings of the divine order are for you. I pray that if there are any who have turned to their own way and have made God second, they will come to repentance on all lines. Separate yourself from every earthly touch, and touch ideas. And God will bring you to an end of yourself. Begin with God this moment.

The Way to Overcome: Believe!

First Published in Flames of Fire p. 2 March 1917

First John 5. The greatest weakness in the world is unbelief. The greatest power is the faith that worketh by love. Love, mercy, and grace are bound eternally to faith. There is no fear in love and no question as to being caught up when Jesus comes. The world is filled with fear, torment, remorse, and brokenness, but faith and love are sure to overcome. "Who is he that overcometh the world, but he that believeth that Jesus is the Son of God?" (1 John 5:5). God hath established the earth and humanity on the lines of faith. As you come into line, fear is cast out, the Word of God comes into operation and you find bedrock. The way to overcome is to believe Jesus is the Son of God. The commandments are wrapped up in it.

When there is a fidelity between you and God and the love of God is so real that you feel you could do anything for Jesus, all the promises are yea and amen to those who believe. Your life is centered there. Always overcoming what is in the world.

Who keepeth the commandments? The born of God. "Ye are of God, little children, and have overcome them: because greater is he that is in you, than he that is in the world" (1 John 4:4). They that believe, love. When did He love us? When we were in the mire. What did He say? Thy sins are forgiven thee. Why did He say it? Because He loved us. What for? That He might bring many sons into glory. His object? That we might be with Him forever. All the pathway is an education for this high vocation and calling. This hidden mystery of love to us, the undeserving! For our sins the double blessing. "...whatsoever is born of God overcometh the world: and this is the victory...even our faith" (1 John 5:4). He who believeth — to believe is to overcome. On the way to Emmaus Jesus, beginning from Moses and all the prophets, interpreted to them in all the Scriptures the things concerning Himself (Luke 24:27). He is the root! In Him is life. When we receive Christ, we receive God and the promises (Galatians 3:29), that we might receive the promise of the Spirit through faith. I am heir to all the promises because I believe. A great heirship! I overcome because I believe the truth. The truth makes me free.

TONGUES AND INTERPRETATION: "It is God who exalteth, God who maketh rich. The Lord in His mighty arms bears thee up — it is the Lord that encompasseth round about thee. When I am weak, then I am strong."

No wavering! This is the principle. He who believes is definite, and because Jesus is in it, it will come to pass. He is the same yesterday, today, and forever (Hebrews 13:8). They that are poor in spirit are heirs to all. There is no limit to the power, for God is rich to all who call upon Him. Not the will of the flesh, but of God (John 1:13). Put in your claim for your children, your families, your co-workers, that many sons may be brought to glory (Hebrews 2:10), for it is all on the principle of faith. There is nothing in my life or ambition equal to my salvation, a spiritual revelation from heaven according to the power of God, and it does not matter how many flashlights Satan sends through the human mind; roll all on the blood. Who overcomes? He who believes Jesus is the Son (1 John 5:5). God calls in the person with no credentials, it's the order of faith, He who believeth overcometh — will be caught up. The Holy Ghost gives revelation all along the line. He that is not against us is for us, and some of the most godly have not touched Pentecost yet. We must have a good heart especially to the household of faith. "...If any man love the world, the love of the Father is not in him" (1 John 2:15). The root principle of all truth in the human heart is Christ, and when grafted deeply there are a thousand lives you may win. Jesus is the way, the truth, and the life (John 14:6), the secret to every hard problem in the world.

You can't do it! Joseph could not! Everything depends on the principles in your heart. If God dwells in us the principle is light, it comprehends darkness. If thine eye be single, thy whole body shall be full of light, breaking through the hardest thing. "Herein is our love made perfect, that we may have boldness in the day of judgment: because as he is, so are we in this world (1 John 4:17) — for faith has full capacity. When man is pure and it is easy to detect darkness, he that hath this hope purifieth himself (1 John 3:3).

TONGUES AND INTERPRETATION: "God confirms in us faith that we may be refined in the world, having neither spot nor blemish nor any such thing. It is all on the line of faith, he that hath faith overcomes — it is the Lord Who purifieth and bringeth where the fire burns up all the dross, and anoints with fresh oil; see to it that ye keep pure. God is separating us for Himself.

"...I will give you a mouth and wisdom, which all your adversaries will not be able to gainsay nor resist" (Luke 21:15). The Holy Spirit will tell you in the moment what you shall say. The world will not understand you, and you will find as you go on with God that you do not under-stand fully. We cannot comprehend what we are saved to, or from. None can express the joy of God's indwelling. The Holy Spirit can say through you the need of the moment. The world knoweth us not because it knew Him not.

"Who is he that overcometh the world, but he that believeth Jesus is the Son of God?" (1 John 5:5). A place of confidence in God, a place of prayer, a place of knowledge, that we have what we ask, because we keep His commandments and do the things that are pleasing in His sight. Enoch before his translation had the testimony, he had been well-pleasing unto God. We overcome by believing.

Our Calling, part 1

Message given at Glad Tidings Tabernacle and Bible Training School, 1536, Ellis Street, San Francisco, California August 18, 1922

I want to speak to you this morning from the fourth chapter of Ephesians. We will begin reading from the first verse:

I therefore, the prisoner of the Lord, beseech you that ye walk worthy of the vocation wherewith ye are called, With all lowliness and meekness, with longsuffering, forbearing one another in love; Endeavoring to keep the unity of the Spirit in the bond of peace. There is one body, and one Spirit, even as ye are called in one hope of your calling; One Lord, one faith, one baptism, One God and Father of all, who is above all, and through all, and in you all. But unto every one of us is given grace according to the measure of the gift of Christ. Wherefore he saith, When he ascended up on high, he led captivity captive, and gave gifts unto men. (Now that he ascended, what is it but that he also descended first into the lower parts of the earth? He that descended is the same also that ascended up far above all heavens, that he might fill all things.) And he gave some, apostles; and some, prophets; and some, evangelists; and some, pastors and teachers; For the perfecting of the saints, for the work of the ministry, for the edifying of the body of Christ: Till we all come in the unity of the faith, and of the knowledge of the Son of God, unto a perfect man, unto the measure of the stature of the fullness of Christ. Ephesians 4:1-13

Beloved, we have for several mornings been speaking concerning the gifts. And I believe that the Lord would have us this morning further consider another side of the gifts. I shall be more or less speaking to preachers, and to those who desire to be preachers. I would like to utter those same words Paul utters in 1 Corinthians 14:5:

I would that ye all spoke with tongues, but rather that ye prophesied...

I believe there is no way to make proclamation but by the Spirit. And I believe that they that are sent are called and chosen of God to be sent. And so as we go forth into this chapter, I trust that everyone will understand what his vocation is in the Spirit, and what the Lord demands of us as preachers.

We should be able in the face of God and the presence of His people to behave ourselves so comely and pleasing to the Lord that we always leave behind us a life of blessing and power without gendering strife.

It is a great choice to become a preacher of the Gospel, to handle the Word of life. We that handle the Word of life ought to be well built on the lines of common sense, judgment, and not given to anything which is contrary to the Word of God. There should be in us all the time such deep reverence towards God and His Word that under all circumstances we would not forfeit our principles on the lines of faith that God had revealed unto us by the truth.

Today I believe God will show us how wonderful we may be in the order of the Spirit for God wants us to be always in the Spirit so rightly dividing the Word of truth that all who hear it shall be like strength to weakness. It shall bring oil to the troubled heart. It shall bring rest. The Word of God shall make us know that having done all we may stand in the trial.

God would have us to know that there is strength by the power of the Spirit, of an equipment of character to bring us into like-mindedness with the Lord. We must know to be baptized in the Holy Ghost is to leave your own life, as it were, out of all questioning; leave yourself out of all pleasing, and in the name of Jesus come into like-mindedness.

How He pleased God! How He brought heaven to earth, and all earth moved at the mightiness of the presence of heaven in the midst. We must see our vocation in the Spirit, for God hath chosen us. We must remember that it is a great choice. Turning to the tenth chapter of Romans, we read:

And how shall they preach, except they be sent?...How beautiful are the feet of them that preach the gospel of peace, and bring glad tidings of good things! Romans 10:15

We want to be sent. It is a great thing to be called of God to preach the unsearchable riches of Christ. You have in this land, and we have in our land, men of note and of authority, who are looked to on the lines of socialistic problems. I often think that Lloyd George has a wonderful time but not a time like a preacher. He only preaches of natural sources but the man who handles the Word of God preaches life immortality that swallows up life. When we come into this blessed life we know we are teaching principles and ideals which are for life eternal.

God has given to us in the Spirit, and behold, we are spiritual children today, and we must know that we have to be spiritual all the time. God forbid that we should ever be like the Galatian church, after we have been in the Spirit, we could come in the flesh. You are allowed to go into the Spirit but you are never allowed to come in the flesh after you have been in the Spirit.

And so God gives such an idea of this high order in the Spirit that we may be moved by its power to see how we may change strength and come into all the line of faith in God. Let me turn to the first verse of this wonderful fourth chapter of Ephesians:

I therefore, the prisoner of the Lord, beseech you that ye walk worthy of the vocation wherewith ye are called.

Here is Paul in prison. If I can take a word from anybody, I can take it from anyone who is in prison. I have never read a book but the Bible, but there are some things I have read out of Pilgrims Progress which have helped me very much. It was when he was in prison that God wakened him on so many wonderful lines of thought. How Paul must have read the Word right in the hearts of those who came and went when he was bound with chains for two full years. He could speak about a fullness, freedom, power, and joy although he was bound with chains.

My brothers, there is something in the Gospel different from anything else. And if these men could go through such hardships – read the first epistle of Peter and you will see how they were scattered. God says that the world wasn't worthy of such material as God was filling with His power that were in dens and caves of the earth.

Oh brother and sister, there have been some wonderful gems passed through the world touched by the Master's hand. There have been some wonderful men in the world who have caught the glory as the rays have shone from His lips by the power of His expression. As they beheld Him they have been fascinated with Him. And I can fairly see as Peter drew near the time of his departure, as Jesus said:

...When thou wast young, thou girdedst thyself, and walkedst whither thou wouldest: but when thou shalt be old, thou shalt stretch forth thy hands, and another shall gird thee, and carry thee whither thou wouldest not. John 21:18

And as Peter drew near to the portals of glory, he wished to die with his head downwards. My word! What grace incarnated in a human casket that it should have such ideals of worship.

Oh, beloved, God is a real essence of joy to us in a time when it seems barrenness, when it seems nothing can help us but the light from heaven far above the brightness of the sun. Then that touches you, then that changes you, and you realize nothing is worthwhile but that.

How he speaks to us when he is in prison, about "the vocation wherewith ye are called, with all lowliness and meekness" (Ephesians 4:1,2). He speaks unto the preacher. Let no person in this place think that he cannot become a preacher. Let none think he cannot reach this ideal of lowliness and meekness. God can bring us there.

Some preachers get an idea that nobody ought to say a word till they are established. I like to hear the bleating of the lambs. I like to hear the life of the young believer. I like to hear something coming right from heaven into the soul as they rise the first time with tears coming down their eyes, telling of the love of Jesus.

The Holy Ghost fell upon a young man outside a church. He went into the church where they were all so sedate. If anything had to move in that church out of the ordinary, my word! It would be extraordinary. And this young man with his fullness of life and zeal for the Master got into ejaculating and praising the Lord, and making manifest the joy of the Lord, and he disturbed the old saints.

An old man one day was reading the Psalms quietly. It touched a young man sitting behind him who was filled with the Holy Ghost, And the young man shouted, "Glory!" Said the old man, "Do you call that religion?"

The father of the young man to whom we referred was one of the deacons of the church. The other deacons got round him and said, "You must talk to your boy, and give him to understand that he has to wait till he is established before he manifests those things."

So his father had a long talk with the boy, and told him what the deacons said. "You know," he said, "I must respect the deacons, and they have told me they won't hate this thing. You have to wait till you are established."

As they neared their home their horse made a full stop. He tried to make it go forward and back but the horse would not move for anything.

What is up with the horse?" asked the father of the son. "Father," replied the boy, "this horse has got established."

I pray God the Holy Ghost that we will not get established in that way. God, loose us up from these old, critical, long-faced, poisoned kind of countenances, which haven't seen daylight for many days. They come into the sanctuary and are in a terrible way. May the

Lord save Pentecost from going to dry rot. Yea, deliver us from any line of sentimentality, anything which is not reality. For remember, we must have reality of supernatural quickening till we are sane and active, and not in any way dormant, but filled with life, God working in us mightily by His Spirit.

We must always be on the transforming position, not on the conforming condition, always renewing the mind, always renovated by the mighty thoughts of God, always being brought into line with that which God has said to us by the Spirit, "This is the way, walk ye in it." "Walk in the Spirit, and ye shall not fulfill the lusts of the flesh."

Lord, how shall we do it? Can a man be meek and lowly, and filled with joy? Do they work together? "Out of the abundance of the heart the mouth speaketh." The depths of God come in, in lowliness and meekness and make the heart love. There is no heart can love like the heart that God has touched.

Oh, that love that is made to love the sinner! There is no love like it. I always feel I can spend any time with the sinner. Oh, brother, there is a love which is God's love! There is a love which only comes by the principles of the Word of God. "He loved us and gave Himself for us."

When that meekness and lowliness of mind take hold, the preacher is moved by His Creator to speak from heart to heart and move the people. For without we are moved by an inward power and ideal of principles, we are never worth. We must have ideals which come from the throne of God. We must live in the throne, live on the throne, and let Him be enthroned, and then He will lift us to the throne.

TONGUES AND INTERPRETATION: "Out of the depths He has called us, into the heights He has brought us, unto the uttermost He has saved us to make us kings and priests unto God. For we are His property, His own, His loved ones. Therefore He wants to clothe us upon, with the gifts of the Spirit, and make us worthy for His ministry."

Glory to God! Thank the Lord!

"With all lowliness and meekness, with longsuffering, forbearing one another in love" (Ephesians 4:2).

Oh, how it is needed, "forbearing one another in love." Oh, how this is contrary to hardness of heart; how this is contrary to the evil powers; how this is contrary to the natural mind. It is a divine revelation, and you cannot forbear till you know how He has been with you in the same thing. It is God's love toward you that makes tender, compassionate love one toward another.

It is only the broken, contrite heart which has received the mark of God. It is only those in that secluded place where He speaks to thee alone, and encourages thee when thou art down and out, and when no hand is stretched out to thee, He stretches out His hand with mercy and brings thee into a place of compassion. And now, you cannot think evil; now you cannot in any way act hard. God has brought you into long-suffering, with tenderness, with love.

Oh, this love, brother! Many a time my two brothers have been under conviction and have wept under conviction as I have tried to bring them into the light. But up till now neither of them is in the light. I believe God will bring them.

In the church of God, where a soul is on fire, kindled with the love of God, there is a deeper love between me and that brother than there is between me and my earthly brother. Oh, this love that I am speaking about is divine love, it is not human love. It is higher than human love, it is more devoted to God. It will not betray. It is true in everything. You can depend upon it. It won't change its character. It will be exactly as He would act for you will act with the same spirit, for as He is so are ye in this world.

As you rise into association with Him in the Spirit, as you walk with Him in the light as He is in the Light, then the fellowship becomes unique in all its plan. I pray God that He will help us to understand it that we shall be able to put off and put on. We shall be able to be clothed upon as we have never been, with another majestic touch, with another ideal of heaven.

No one can love like God. And when He takes us into this divine love we shall exactly understand this Word, this verse, for it is full of entreaty, it is full of passion and compassion, it has every touch of Jesus right in it. It is so lovely:

"With all lowliness and meekness, with longsuffering, forbearing one another in love."

Isn't it glorious? You cannot find it anywhere else. You cannot get these pictures in any place you go to. I challenge you to go into any library in the world and find words coined or brought forth like these words, without they are copied from this Word. It isn't in nature's garden, it is in God's. It is the Spirit explaining, for He alone can explain this ideal of beatitudes. They are marvelous, they are beautiful, they are full of grandeur, they are God's. Hallelujah!

I hope you are having a good time, for it is just filling me with new wine this morning. Oh, it is lovely!

"Endeavoring to keep the unity of the Spirit in the bond of peace" (Ephesians 4:3).

This is one of the main principles of this chapter. Beloved, let us keep in mind this very thought today. I am speaking this morning, by the grace of God, to the preacher. It should never be known that any preacher caused any distraction, or detraction, or any split, or disunion in a meeting. The preacher has lost his unction and his glory if he ever stoops to anything that would weaken the assembly in any way.

The greatest weakness of any preacher is to draw men to himself. It is a fascinating point, but you must be away from fascination. If you don't crucify your "old man" on every line, you are not going into divine lines with God. When they wanted to make Jesus king, He withdrew Himself to pray. Why? It was a human desire of the people. What did He want? His Kingdom was a spiritual Kingdom. He was to reign over demon powers. He was to have power over the passions of human life. He was to reign so supremely over everything which is earthly, that all the people might know He was divine.

He is our pattern, beloved. When they want to make anything of us, He will give you grace to refuse it. The way to get out is to find there is nothing in the earth which is worthy of Him; that there is no one in the world who is able to understand but He; that everything will crumble to the dust and become worthless. Only that which is divine will last.

"Be not afraid to ask, because God is on the throne waiting to answer your request."

Every time you draw anyone to yourself it has a touch of earth. It does not speak of the highest realm of thought of God. There is something about it which cannot bear the light of the Word of God. Keep men's eyes off you, but get their eyes on the Lord. Live in the world without a touch or taint of any natural thing moving you. Live high in the order and authority of God, and see that everything is bearing you on to greater heights and depths and greater knowledge of the love of God.

You will help any assembly you go to, and everybody will get a blessing and will see how much richer they are because you brought them Jesus. Only Jesus! And He is too big for any assembly, and He is little enough to fill every heart. We will always go on to learn of Him. Whatever we know, the knowledge is so small to what He has to give us. And so God's plan for us in giving us Jesus, is all things, for all things consist in Him.

"All things were made by him; and without him was not anything made that was made" (John 1:3).

"...in him we live, and move, and have our being..." (Acts 17:28).

And when it is a spiritual being and an activity of holiness, see how wonderfully we grow in the Lord. Oh, it is just lovely!

TONGUES AND INTERPRETATION: "Yea, it is the Lord Himself. He comes forth clothed upon to clothe thee in thy weakness, to strengthen thee in thy helplessness, to uphold thee in the limitation of thy knowledge, to unfold the mysteries of the Kingdom in the dire straits where two ways meet, and you know not where to go. He says, 'This is the way.' When thou art in such a straitened place that no hand but God is able to lead thee out, then He comes to thee and says, 'Be strong and fear not, for I am with thee.'"

Hallelujah! Praise the Lord of glory! He is the everlasting King, and will reign forever and ever and ever. Glory! Glory! Amen!

TONGUES AND INTERPRETATION: "God has spoken and He will make it clear, for He is in the midst of thee to open out thy mind and reveal unto thee all the mysteries of the Kingdom, for the God of grace is with thee. For God is greater than all unto thee. He is making thy way straight before thee, for the Lord is He that comforteth thee as He comforted Israel, and will lead thee into His power, for His right hand is with thee to keep thee in all thy ways lest thou shouldst dash thy foot against a stone, for the Lord will uphold thee."

How beautiful is the Scripture coming to us this morning! How lively it appears to us! And now we can understand something about the fourteenth chapter of First Corinthians:

...I will pray with the spirit, and I will pray with the understanding also: I will sing with the spirit, and I will sing with the understanding also. Verse 15

So God is bringing us right into the fullness of the Pentecostal power as given in the first days. God wants us t know that after we have been brought into this divine life with Christ, we are able to speak in the Spirit, and we are able to sing in the Spirit; we are able to speak with the understanding, and sing with the understanding also. Ah, hallelujah this good day!

I think I ought to say a few more words concerning: "Endeavoring to keep the unity of the Spirit in the bond of peace" (Ephesians 4:3).

Beloved, I want you, above all things, to remember that the church is one body. She has many members, and we are all members of that one body. At any cost we must not break up the body but rather keep the body in perfect unity. Never try to get the applause of the people by any natural thing. Yours is a spiritual work. Yours has to be a spiritual breath. Your word has to be the Word of God. Your counsel to the church has to be so that it cannot be gainsaid. You have to have such solid, holy reverence on every line so that every time you handle anybody you handle them for God, and you handle the church as the church of God. By that means you keep the church bound together.

As the church is bound together in one Spirit, they grow into that temple in the Lord, and they all have one voice, one desire, and one plan. And when they want souls saved, they are all of one mind. I am speaking now about spiritual power. You get them into the mind of the Spirit with Christ, and all their desires will be the same desires of Christ the Head. And so nothing can break the church on those lines.

As preachers you must never try to save yourself on any line. You must always be above mentioning a financial matter on your side. Always before God in the secret place mention your need, but never bring it to an assembly; if you do, you drop in the estimation of the assembly. You are allowed to tell any need belonging to the assembly or the church management, but on a personal line never refer to yourself on the platform.

If you preach faith you must live it, and a man is not supposed to preach without he preach a living faith. And he must so impress it upon the people that they will always know God has taken us on for a special plan and that we are not ordinary men. After we are called of God and chosen for Him, we are not again to have ordinary men's plans. We ought to have ideals of God only.

Another thing which I think is perhaps more essential to you than anything else: you preachers, never drop into an assembly and say the Lord sent you, because sometimes the assembly has as much on as she can manage. But it is right for you to get your orders from heaven, and for God to switch the same order somewhere else that will make the first call and you will be dropping into the call. Never make a call without you are really sent. Be sure you are sent of God.

Brothers, can you be out of God's will when you hear His voice? "My sheep hear My voice, and they follow Me." Oh, that God today shall help us by the mind of the Spirit to understand. I believe God has a message on fire. He has men clothed by God. He has men sent by God. Will you be the men? Will you be the women?

You ask, "Can I be the man? Can I be the woman?" Yes, God says, "Many are called, but few are chosen." Are you the chosen ones? Those who desire to be chosen, will you allow God to choose you? Then He will put His hand upon you. And in the choice He will give you wisdom, He will lead you forth, He will stand by you in the straitened corner, He will lead you every step of the way, for the Lord's anointed shall go forth and bring forth fruit, and their fruit shall remain.

TONGUES AND INTERPRETATION: "Behold, now is the day of decision. Yield now while the moment of pressure by the presence of God comes. Yield now and make your consecration to God."

The altar is ready now for all who will obey.

Our Calling, part 2

Message given at Glad Tidings Tabernacle and Bible Training School, 1536, Ellis Street, San Francisco, California August 22, 1922

TONGUES AND INTERPRETATION: "The Lord is that Spirit that moves in the regenerated, and brings us to the place where fire can begin and burn, and separate, and transform, and make you all know that God has made an inroad into every order. Because we have to be divine, spiritual, changed, and on fire to catch all the rays of His life, first, burning out; second, transforming; and third, making you fit to live or die."

Oh, thank God for that interpretation.

I want to turn your attention again to the fourth chapter of Ephesians, to continue our subject of last week. I will read from the first verse:

I therefore, the prisoner of the Lord, beseech you that ye walk worthy of the vocation wherewith ye are called, with all lowliness and meekness, with longsuffering, forbearing one another in love; Endeavoring to keep the unity of the Spirit in the bond of peace. There is one body, and one Spirit, even as ye are called in one hope of your calling; One Lord, one faith, one baptism. One God and Father of all, who is above all and through all and in you all. But unto every one of us is given grace according to the measure of the gift of Christ. Wherefore he saith, When he ascended up on high, he led captivity captive, and gave gifts unto men. (Now that he ascended, what is it but that he also descended first into the lower parts of the earth? He that descended is the same also that ascended up far above all heavens, that he might fill all things.) And he gave some, apostles; and some, prophets; and some, evangelists; and some, pastors and teachers; For the perfecting of the Saints, for the work of the ministry, for the edifying of the body of Christ: Till we all come in the unity of the faith, and of the knowledge of the Son of God, unto a perfect man, unto the measure of the stature of the fullness of Christ. Ephesians 4:1-13

I believe the Lord, this morning as on the last morning, especially wants me to emphasize facts which will be a blessing and a strengthening to the preachers. If there is anything of importance it is to the preachers because God must have us in the place of building and edifying the Church. And we must be in that order of the Spirit that God can work through us for the needs of the Church.

As it was only out of the brokenness of Paul's life that blessing came forth, so it is out of the emptiness, and brokenness, and yieldedness of our lives that God can bring forth all His glories through us to others. And as our brother said this morning on the platform, except we pass on what we receive we shall lose it. If we didn't lose it, it would become stagnant.

Virtue is always manifested through blessing which you have passed on. Nothing will be of any importance to you except that which you pass on to others. So God wants us to be so in the order of the Spirit that when He breaks upon us the alabaster box of ointments of His precious anointing which He has for every child of His, He wants us to be filled with perfumes of holy incense that we may be poured out for others and that others may receive the graces of the Spirit, and all the church may be edified. And there shall never be known in Glad Tidings Tabernacle one dry day, but there shall always be freshness and life which makes all hearts burn together as you know the Lord has talked with you once more.

We must have this inward burning desire for more of God. We must not be at any stationary point. We must always have the highest power telescopes looking and hasting unto that which God has called us to that He may perfect that forever.

Oh, what a blessed inheritance of the Spirit God has for us in these days, that we should be no longer barren, nor unfruitful, but rather filled with all fullness, unlimited, increasing with all increasings, with a measureless measure of the might of the Spirit in the inner man, so that we are always like a great river pressing on and healing everything that it touches. Oh, let it be so today!

TONGUES AND INTERPRETATION: "The Lord has awakened in us the divine touches of His spiritual favor to make us know He is here with all you require if you are ready to take it."

But are we ready to take it? If we are, then God can give us wonderful things. We must be always in that hunger ready for every touch of God.

Last week you remember we were dwelling on verse three: "Endeavoring to keep the unity of the Spirit in the bond of peace."

It was a very precious word to us because it meant that under any circumstances we would not have our way but God's way. We have it for the person and for the Church.

Whatever God means us to be, He means us to be peacemakers. Yes, love without alloy; that which, always at its own expense, goes to help another and pays the price for it. I shall not find a Scripture which will help me so much on this line as Matthew 5:23,24:

Therefore if thou bring thy gift to the altar; and there rememberest that thy brother hath aught against thee; Leave there thy gift before the altar, and go thy way; first be reconciled to thy brother; and then come and offer thy gift.

Most Christians are satisfied with the first line of it, but the second line is deeper. Most people believe it is perfectly right if you have offended another, to go to that one and say, "Please forgive me," and you gain your brother when you take that part. But this is a deeper sense: "If thou...rememberest that thy brother hath ought against thee," go forgive him his transgressions. It is so much deeper than getting your own side right, to go and get their side right by forgiving them all they have done.

That will be a stepping stone to very rich grace on the line of "keeping the unity of the Spirit in the bond of peace." Someone says, "I cannot forgive her because she did that, and the brother said that. You know the brother didn't recognize me at all. And he has never smiled at me for at least six months." Poor thing! God help you through evil report and good report. God can take us right through if we get to the right side of grace.

My brother, when you get to the place of forgiving your brother who hath ought against you, you will find that is the greatest ideal of going on to perfection, and the Lord will help us "to keep the unity of the Spirit in the bond of peace."

I like that "bond of peace." It is an inward bond between you and the child of God. "Bond of peace." Hallelujah! Oh, glory to God!

There is one body, and one Spirit, even as ye are called in one hope of your calling. Ephesians 4:4

We must recognize there is only one body. It seems to me that God would at one time have made such an inroad into all nations on the lines of the truth through the Plymouth brethren, if they had only recognized that there was more in the body than just the Plymouth brethren. You will never gain interest without you see that in every church there will be a nucleus which has as real a God as you have.

It is only on these lines I believe that the longsuffering of God waiteth for the precious fruit. And the longsuffering of God is with the believers who have an idea that only those in Glad Tidings

Hall are right, or those in Oakland, or those in England. It is all foolishness.

Fancy people sitting round the table and reckoning that that table is the only table. What about hundreds of people I know who are sitting round the table every day and taking the bread and the wine? Brother, the body of Christ consists of all who are in Christ.

While we know the Holy Ghost is the only power that can take the Church up, we know the Holy Ghost will go with the Church. The Scriptures are very definite in saying that all that are Christ's at His coming will be changed. It doesn't seem to be that we can be all Christ's without something is done, and God will sweep away so many things which are spoiling things. We must get to perfect love, and we will see that God can make even those in Caesar's household our souls, glory to God!

TONGUES AND INTERPRETATION: "It is the Spirit that joins us and makes us one. It is the health of the Spirit that goes through the body that quickens the body and makes it appear as one."

Oh, the body appearing as one body! The same joy, the same peace, the same hope! No division, all one in Christ! What a body! Who can make a body like that? Seems to me that this body is made deep in the cross. Hundreds of people are carrying a cross on watch guard, or around their necks. I could never carry a cross, He has carried the cross, He has borne the shame. I find right there in that atoning blood there is cleansing and purifying, and taking away every dross, and everything that will mar the vessel, and He is making a vessel unto honor fit for the Master's use, joined up in that body, one body.

Let us be careful that we do not in any way defile the body because God is chastening the body and fitly framing it and bringing it together. The body of Christ will rise. You ask, "How will it rise?" It will rise in millions, and billions, and trillions, more than any man can number. It will be a perfect body.

Oh, there is one body! Ah, it is a lovely body. I look at you, I see you. I look in your faces and I know there is a closer association than one can tell or speak about. Oh, brother, there is something deeper down in the spirit of the regenerated person when the dross of life and the flesh falls off.

Oh, there will be a similitude, a likeness, a perfection of holiness, of love! Oh God, take away the rudiments, the weaknesses, all the depravities.

"Now ye are the body of Christ, and members in particular" (1 Corinthians 12:27).

I like the word, particular, meaning to say there is just the right place for us. God sees us in that place. He is making us fit in that place so that for all time we shall have a wonderful place in that body. Ah, it is so lovely!

Oh, these exhaustless things! Brothers, sisters, it isn't the message, it is the heart. It isn't the heart, it is the Christ. It isn't the Christ, it is the God. It isn't the God, it is the whole Body. Deeper and more precious than we have any conception of!

There is one body, and one Spirit, even as ye are called in one hope of your calling. Ephesians 4:4

I feel that God would have me say a word about the calling. Many people get called and they have missed because they are dull of hearing.

There is something in the call, beloved. "Many are called, but few are chosen." I want a big heart this morning to believe that all shall be chosen. You ask, "Can it be so?" Yes, beloved, it can, not few chosen, but many chosen.

And how shall the choice be? The choice is always your choice first. You will find that gifts are your choice first. You will find that salvation is your choice. God has made it all but you have to choose. And so God wants you especially this morning to make an inward call, to have a great intercessory condition of beseeching the Holy One to prepare you for that wonderful mystical Body.

Called! Beloved, I know some people have an idea (and it is a great mistake), because they are not successful in everything they touch, because they have failed in so many things they have been desirous to go forward in, because they don't seem to aspire in prayer as some, and perhaps don't enter into the fullness of tongues, that there is no hope for them in this calling.

Satan comes and says, "Look at that black catalogue of helpless infirmities! You never expect to be in that calling!" Yes, you can, brother! God has it in the Scriptures. Oh, my brother, it is the weakness made strong! " It is the last that can be made first. What will make the whole different? When we confess our helplessness. He says He feeds the hungry with good things, but the satisfied He sends away empty.

If you want to grow in grace and in the knowledge of the grace of God, get hungry enough to be fed, be thirsty enough to cry, be broken enough you cannot have anything in the world without He comes Himself. I was reading last night in my Bible, it was so lovely, "And God shall wipe away all tears from their eyes..." (Revelation 21:4).

Ah, you say, that will be there. Thank God there are two "theres." Hallelujah! Let God do it this morning. Let Him wipe away all tears. Let Him comfort thy heart. Let Him strengthen thy weakness. Let Him cause thee to come into the place of profit. Let Him help thee into the place God has chosen for thee, for "many are called, but few are chosen." But God has a big choice.

He is a big Jesus! If I could measure Him I would be very small. But I cannot measure Him, and I know He is very large. I am glad I cannot measure Jesus but I am glad I can touch Him all the same. The fifth verse: One Lord, one faith, one baptism. Ephesians 4:5.

I must touch the thought of baptism this morning. We must get away from the thought of water baptism when we are in the epistles. If water baptism is at all mentioned in any way, it is always mentioned as a past tense. We must always remember this, beloved, that while water baptism, in my opinion, is essential, "He that believeth, and is baptized, shall be saved." I wouldn't say for a moment a man could not be saved without he was baptized in water, because it would be contrary to Scripture. Yet I see there is a blending. If we turn to the third chapter of John's gospel we find:

...Except a man be born of water and of the Spirit, he cannot enter into the kingdom of God. John 3:5

I believe God would have us to know that we never ought to put aside water baptism, but believe it is in perfect conjunction and in operation with the working of the Spirit that we may be buried with Him.

But oh, the baptism in the Holy Ghost! The baptism of fire! The baptism of power! The baptism of oneness! The baptism of association! The baptism of communion! The baptism of the Spirit of life which takes the man, shakes him through, builds him up, and makes him know he is a new creature in the Spirit, worshipping God in the Spirit.

If my preaching and the preaching of those who come on this platform emphasizes the facts of being baptized with the Holy Ghost, and you only have touches of it, if you stop at that, you will be almost as though you were missing the calling. John said by the Spirit:

...He that cometh after me is preferred before me.... John 1:15

I indeed baptize you with water unto repentance: but he that cometh after me is mightier than I...he shall baptize you with the Holy Ghost, and with fire. Matthew 3:11

By all means if you can tarry, you ought to tarry. If you have the Spirit's power upon you, go into that room or somewhere else and never cease till God finishes the work. Outside the Pentecostal church where there isn't a revival spirit, and where people are not born again, you will find the church becomes dead, dry, and barren, and helpless. They enter into entertainments and all kinds of teas. They live on a natural association and lose their grand, glorious hope.

I come to the Pentecostal church. Without the Pentecostal church is having an increase on the lines of salvation, without it is having continuous baptisms in the Holy Ghost, and a continuous pressure into the Kingdom, that church will become dry, lukewarm, helpless, and you will wonder what church it is.

But every night if somebody rises up in testimony saying they received the Holy Ghost, and others say, "Oh, last night I was saved," that church is ripening. She will not flounder. She is ripening for greater things, for God will take that church.

Beloved, you are responsible for this, the platform is not responsible. The whole Church is responsible to keep this place on fire. If you have come into this meeting, if you are baptized with the Holy Ghost, without an unction upon you and ready so that you feel like bursting into tongues, or having a psalm, hymn, or some spiritual song, without you have a tongue or interpretation, without something is taking place on these lines you have fallen from the grace of the Pentecostal position.

You talk about a message. God has given us a message this morning if you dare hear it. We dare say in the open air and everywhere that we are Pentecostal. If we are Pentecostal we shall be Biblical Pentecostal. What is Biblical Pentecost? It is found in the fourteenth chapter of First Corinthians, 26th verse:

How is it then, brethren? When ye come together every one of you hath a psalm, hath a doctrine, hath a tongue, hath a revelation, hath an interpretation. Let all things be done unto edifying.

It is an injunction for a Pentecostal continuance in the Corinthian church. Supposing that was the case of this Pentecostal church, it would not be possible for sinners to come in without being saved, or for people coming in not having the baptism without having a hunger and thirst to come into that fullness. It must be so. God must bring us to a place where we have not a name, but have the position that brings the name.

How many of you felt speaking in tongues as you came into the room this morning? Praise God, there are some. How many of you have a psalm burning through you and feel like rehearsing it in the streets? Praise God, that is very well. How many of you sung a hymn as you came along? Praise the Lord, glory to God! You are going on very well. But don't you see this is what we have to continue. There has to be a continuance of such things.

TONGUES AND INTERPRETATION: "The hope of the Church is springing up of the Spirit through the Word. Therefore, as many of you as are living in the Spirit are putting to death the flesh. You are quickened by the Spirit and live in the realms of His grace."

Praise the Lord, it is the grace of our Lord Jesus. Hallelujah! We can sing, "I will never be cross anymore." Beloved, it is the most wonderful thing on earth when God touches you with this new life in the Spirit. Oh, then whether you are on the streets, or roadways, or trains, it doesn't matter where, you are in the Spirit, you are ready to be caught up.

Oh, beloved, here we are this morning, "one body," praise the Lord! One spirit, one baptism. I am crying to God for these meetings because I believe God can do a great thing in a moment when we are all brought into line of the Spirit. It wouldn't surprise me whatever happened.

I have been in meetings for ten days when the attention has been on the gifts, and the people have gotten so worked up, as it were, in the Spirit that they felt something had to happen on a new line else they couldn't live. And it has happened. I believe these and other meetings are bringing us to a place of great expectancy. "One Lord, one faith, one baptism" (Ephesians 4:5).

Just in the proportion that you have the Spirit unfolding to you, "One Lord, one faith, one baptism," you have the Holy Ghost so incarnated in you bringing into you a revelation of the Word. Nothing else can do it, for the Spirit gave the Word through Jesus. Jesus spoke by the Spirit that was in Him, He being the Word. The Spirit brought out all the Word of this life. Then we must have the Spirit.

If you take up John's gospel you will find that when He came it wasn't to speak about Himself but to bring forth all He said. Just as we have the measure of the Spirit, there will be no measure of unbelief. We shall have faith. The Church will rise to the highest position when there is no schism in the Body of the lines of unbelief. When we all, with one heart, and one faith, believe the Word as it is spoken, then signs, and wonders, and divers miracles will be manifested everywhere. One accord: "One Lord, one faith, one baptism." Hallelujah!

The next verse I think probably is one of the primary verses of all:

One God and Father of all, who is above all, and through all, and in you all. Ephesians 4:6

If this spiritual life be in us, we will find we have no fear. We would have no nervous debility, it would vanish. Every time you have fear, it is imperfect love. Every time you have nervous weaknesses, you will find it is a departing from an inner circle of true faith in God. We read in 1 John 4:18:

There is no fear in love; but perfect love casteth out fear: because fear hath torment. He that feareth is not made perfect in love.

Then you can get a very good word in the sixteenth verse of the same chapter:

...God is love; and he that dwelleth in love dwelleth in God, and God in him.

Where is the man? He is swallowed up in God. And when God takes hold of us on these lines it is remarkable to see we are encircled and overshadowed by Him.

TONGUES AND INTERPRETATION: "I feel we must magnify the Lord in the Spirit."

When the believer sees that God is over all, take a real glance at that. Think about God being through all. See if any satanic powers can work against you. But just think about another step; He is in you all. How can the devil have a chance with the body when God is "in you all"? Hallelujah! Glory!

Don't you see the groundwork, the great base, the rock of the principles of these Scriptures, how they make us know that we are not barren, we cannot be unfruitful, but we must always be abounding and in the joy of the Lord. We lack because we are short of truth.

When this truth of God lays hold the man, he is no longer a man. What is he? He is a divine construction. He has a new perception of the ideals of God. He has a new measurement. Now he sees God is over all things. Now he sees that God is through all things. The whole world can join in a league of nations, they can do as they like, but the Word of God abideth forever.

"In you all." Think of that, God is in you all. Who is God? Who is the Holy Spirit? Who is Jesus? Is it possible to have any conception of the mightiness of the power of God? And yet you take the thoughts of Jesus ,and see that all the embodiment of the fullness was right in Him. And I have Him. I have the Holy Ghost also which is as great in equality for those three are one, and joined equally in power. They never twaddle on their conditions but are perfectly one.

When the Spirit comes in the body, how many are there in the body? You have Jesus already. When you are baptized you have the Holy Ghost. And now God is in you all. Hallelujah! Talk about Samson carrying the gates, if you know your position you will take both the city and the gates. Go in and possess every part of the land, for surely there is a land of gladness, a land of pleasure, a land of peace, And remember, brothers; when the Holy Ghost gets an end of us, and we just utter the Spirit's power and the Spirit's words, we find out it is always more and more and more. Oh, yes, we will magnify the Lord on all these lines. If we don't the stones will begin to cry out against us.

But unto every one of us is given grace according to the measure of the gift of Christ. Ephesians 4:7

This is a great summing up. Oh, brother, I wish you to see Jesus this morning because if we don't see Him we miss a great deal. Grace and gifts are equally abounding there. It is as you set your strength on Jesus, it is as you allow the Holy Ghost to penetrate every thought bringing always on the canvas of the mind a perfect picture of holiness, purity, righteousness, that you enter into Him and become entitled to all the riches of God.

How do you measure up this morning? God gives a measure. Oh, this is a lovely word:

But unto every one of us is given grace according to the measure of the gift of Christ. Ephesians 4:7

I know that salvation, while it is a perfect work, is an insulation which may have any amount of volts behind it. In the time when they laid bare wires, when they were getting electric power from Niagara, they tell me there was a city whose lights suddenly went out. Following the wires they came to a place where a cat had gotten on the wires, and the lights were stopped. I find that the dynamo of heaven can be stopped with a less thing than a cat. An impure thought across the mind stops the circulation. An act stops the growth of the believer. I like Hebrews 4:12:

For the word of God is quick, and powerful, and sharper than any two edged sword, piercing even to the dividing asunder of soul and spirit, and of the joints and marrow, and is a discerner of the thoughts and intents of the heart.

Then I find in 2 Corinthians 10:5 these words:

Casting down imaginations, and every high thing that exalteth itself against the knowledge of God, and bringing into captivity every thought to the obedience of Christ.

So I find if I am going to have all the revelations of Jesus brought to me, I am going to attain to all that God has for me through a pure heart, a clean heart, right thoughts, and an inward affection towards Him. Then heaven bursts through my human frame, and all the rays of heaven flow through my body. Hallelujah! My word, it is lovely!

The measure of the gift of Christ remains with you. I cannot go on with inspiration without I am going on with God in perfection. I cannot know the mind of the natural and the mysteries of the hidden things with God without I have power to penetrate everything between me and heaven. And there is nothing goes through but a pure heart, for the pure in heart shall see God.

Oh, it is lovely! And I see that the pure heart can come into such closeness with God that the graces are so enriched, and the measure of Christ becomes so increased that you know you are going on to possess all things.

Nothing comes up in my mind so beautiful as a soul just developing in their first love to want to preach to all people. In Revelation, one church is reproved for having lost its first love. And I believe that God would have us to know that this first love, the great love which Jesus gives us with which to love others, is the primary stepping stone to all these things that we had this morning. I don't know whether there is such a one here who has never lost that first love.

The preacher, I love him. The young man I love. Oh, how I love the youth who is developing in his character and longing to become a preacher. If you ask me if I have a choice in my whole life, I say, yes, I have a choice for a young preacher. I love them. God has perfect positions of development for the preacher.

The young preacher may have greater inward longings to get people saved than he has power over his depravities. And they are hindered in their pursuit into this grandeur of God. I want to take you to a place where there is wonderful safety and security.

God will take into captivity him who is captive to weaknesses, and to failures, and to the power of Satan which has interfered with the young or old life that is longing to preach the glories of Christ. God will take him into captivity if he will let Him for God has gifts for him. He takes the captive into captivity and surrounds him, keeps him, chastens him, purifies him, cleanses him, washes him. And He is making prophets of such, and apostles of such, and evangelists of such.

God has never been able to make goodness only out of helplessness lest we should glorify through the flesh. God destroys every line of flesh that no flesh can glory in His sight. If we have any glory, we will glory in the Lord.

Do you want to be preachers? Nay, verily, I know you do. There isn't a child in this place who does not want to bear the glad tidings.

...How beautiful are the feet of them that preach the gospel of peace, and bring glad tidings of good things! Romans 10:15

Oh, glad tidings! What does it mean? Eternal salvation. You talk about gold mines, and diamonds, and precious stones! Oh, my brother, to save one soul from death! Oh, to be the means of saving many! God has for us a richer treasure than we have any idea of. Don't say you cannot reach it, brother, sister. Never look at yourself, get a great vision of the Master. Let His love so penetrate you that you will absolutely make everything death but Him. And as you see Him in His glory, you will see how God can take you.

I believe that there are many in this place that God is taking hold of this morning. My brother, don't fail God, but by the measure of faith in Christ let your hand be outstretched, let your eye be fixed with an eternal fixedness, let an inward passion grip you with the same zeal that took the Lord. And let your mind forget all the past, come into like-mindedness with Jesus and let Him clothe you.

Wherefore he saith, When he ascended up on high, he led captivity captive, and gave gifts unto men. Ephesians 4: 8

He has gifts for men. You ask, what kind of men? Rebels also. Did they desire to be rebels? No. Sometimes there are transgressions who break our hearts and make us groan and traveil. Was it our desire? No. God looks right through the very canvas of your whole life history, and He has set His mind upon you. I would like you preachers to know:

...Eye hath not seen, nor ear heard, neither have entered into the heart of man, the things which God hath prepared for them that love him. 1 Corinthians 2: 9

Your weakness has to be riddled through like the chaff before the wind, and every corn shall bring forth pure grain after God's mind. So the fire will burn as an oven, and burn up the stubble, but the wheat shall be gathered into the garner, the treasury of the most High God, and He Himself shall lay hold of us.

What is it for? The perfecting of the saints. Oh, to think that that brokenness of thine is to be so made like Him, that weakness of thine to be made so strong like Him! Thou hast to bear the image of the Lord in every iota. We have to have the mind of Christ in perfection, in beauty.

Beloved, don't fail and shrivel because of the hand of God upon thee, but think that God must purify thee for the perfecting of the saints. Oh, Jesus will help us this morning. Oh, beloved, what are you going to do with this golden opportunity, with this inward pressure of a cry of God in thy soul? Are you going to let others be crowned, and you lose the crown? Are you willing to be brought into captivity today for God?

Verily, this morning must decide some things. If you are not baptized you must seek the baptism of the Spirit of God. And if there is anything which has marred the fruit, or interfered with all His plan, I beseech you this morning to let the blood so cover, let the anointing of Christ so come, let the vision of Christ so be seen that you will have a measure that shall take all that God has for you.

Ye are Our Epistle, part 1

A two-part message given the same morning at Glad Tidings Tabernacle and Bible Training School, 1536, Ellis Street, San Francisco, California August 23, 1922

I want to read to you this morning the third chapter of Second Corinthians:

Do we begin again to commend ourselves? or need we, as some others, epistles of commendation to you, or letters of commendation from you? Ye are our epistle written in our hearts, known and read of all men: Forasmuch as ye are manifestly declared to be the epistle of Christ ministered by us, written not with ink, but with the Spirit of the living God not in tables of stone, but in fleshy tables of the heart. And such trust have we through Christ to Godward: Not that we are sufficient of ourselves to think anything as of ourselves but our sufficiency is of God; Who also hath made us able ministers of the new testament; not of the letter, but of the spirit: for the letter killeth, but the spirit giveth life. But if the ministration of death, written and engraved in stones, was glorious, so that the children of Israel could not steadfastly behold the face of Moses for the glory of his countenance; which glory was to be done away: How shall not the ministration of the spirit be rather glorious? For if the ministration of condemnation be glory, much more doth the ministration of righteousness exceed in glory, For even that which was made glorious had no glory in this respect, by reason of the glory that excelleth. For if that which is done away was glorious, much more that which remaineth is glorious. Seeing then that we have such hope, we use great plainness of speech: And not as Moses, which put a veil over his face, that the children of Israel could not steadfastly look to the end of that which is abolished: But their minds were blinded: for until this day remaineth the same veil untaken away in the reading of the Old Testament; which veil is done away in Christ. But even unto this day, when Moses is read, the veil is upon their heart. Nevertheless when it shall turn to the Lord, the veil shall be taken away. Now the Lord is that Spirit: and where the Spirit of the Lord is, there is liberty. But we all, with open face beholding as in a glass the glory of the

Lord, are changed into the same image from glory to glory, even as by the Spirit of the Lord. 2 Corinthians 3:1-18

We have this morning one of those high water marks of very deep things of God in the Spirit. I believe the Lord will reveal to us these truths as our hearts are open and responsive to the Spirit's leadings.

But let not any man think he shall receive anything of the Lord only on the lines of a spiritual revelation, for there is nothing that will profit you, or bring you to a place of blessing except that which denounces or brings to death the natural order that the supernatural plan of God may be in perfect order in you.

The Lord of hosts camps round about us this morning, with songs of deliverance that we may see face to face the glories of His grace in a new way, for God hath not brought us into cunningly devised fables but in these days He is rolling away the mists and clouds, and every difficulty that we may understand the mind and will of God.

If we are going to catch the best of God, there must be in this meeting a spiritual desire, the open ear, the understanding heart. The veil must be lifted. We must see the Lord in that perfectness of being glorified in the midst of us. As we enter into these things of the Spirit we must clearly see that we are not going to be able to understand these mysteries that God is unfolding to us, only on the lines of being filled with the Spirit.

Even when these special meetings close, the pastor and everybody else will find that we must all the time grow in grace. We must see that God has nothing for us on the old lines. The new plan, the new revelation, the new victories are before us. The ground must be gained, supernatural things must be attained. All carnal things, and evil powers, and spiritual wickedness in high places must be dethroned. We must come into the line of the Spirit by the will of God in these days.

Let us just turn to the Word which is so beautiful and so expressive in so many ways.

Do we begin again to commend ourselves? Or need we, as some others, epistles of commendation to you, or letters of commendation from you? Ye are our epistle written in our hearts, known and read of all men: Forasmuch as ye are manifestly declared to be the epistle of Christ ministered by us, written not with ink, but with the Spirit of the living God; not in tables of stone, but in fleshy tables of the heart. And such trust have we through Christ to Godward. 2 Corinthians 3:1-4

I want this morning to dwell upon these words for a short time: "Forasmuch as ye are manifestly declared to be the epistle of Christ."

What an ideal position that now the sons of God are being manifested; now the glory is being seen; now the Word of God is becoming an expressed purpose in life till the life has ceased and the Word has begun to live in them.

How truly this position was in the life of Paul when he came to a climax when he said: "I am crucified with Christ: nevertheless I live; yet not I, but Christ liveth in me: and the life which I now live in the flesh I live by the faith of the Son of God, who loved me, and gave himself for me" (Galatians 2:20).

How can Christ live in you? There is no way for Christ to live in you only by the manifested Word in you, through you, manifestly declaring every day that you are a living epistle of the Word of God. Beloved, God would have us to see that no man is perfected or equipped on any lines only as the living Word abides in Him.

It is the living Christ, it is the divine likeness to God, it is the express image of Him, and the Word is the only factor that works out in you and brings forth these glories of identification between you and Christ. It is the Word dwelling in your hearts, richly by faith.

We may begin at Genesis, go right through the Pentateuch, and the other Scriptures, and be able to rehearse them, but without they are a living factor within us, they will be a dead letter. Everything that comes to us must be quickened by the Spirit. "The letter killeth, but the Spirit giveth life."

We must have life in everything. Who knows how to pray but as the Spirit prayeth? What kind of prayer does the Spirit pray? The Spirit always brings to your remembrance the mind of the Scriptures, and brings forth all your cry and your need better than your words. The Spirit always takes the Word of God and brings your heart, and mind, and soul, and cry, and need into the presence of God.

So we are not able to pray only as the Spirit prays, and the Spirit only prays according to the will of God, and the will of God is all in the Word of God. No man is able to speak according to the mind of God and bring forth the deep things of God out of his own mind. The following Scripture rightly divides the Word of truth:

Forasmuch as ye are manifestly declared to be the epistle of Christ ministered by us, written not with ink, but with the Spirit of the living God; not in tables of stone, but in fleshly tables of the heart. 2 Corinthians 3:3

God help us to understand this, for it is out of the heart that all things proceed. When we have entered in with God into the mind of the Spirit, we will find God ravishes our hearts.

Do ye think that the scripture saith in vain, The spirit that dwelleth in us lusteth to envy? James 4:5

I have been pondering over that for years, but now I can see that the Holy Ghost so graciously, so extravagantly, puts everything to one side that He may ravish our hearts with a great inward cry after Jesus. The Holy Spirit "lusteth to envy" for you to have all the divine will of God in Christ Jesus right in your hearts.

When I speak about the "fleshly tables of the heart," I mean the inward love. Nothing is so sweet to me as to know that the heart yearns with compassion. Eyes may see, ears may hear, but you may be immovable on those two lines without you have an inward cry where "deep calleth unto deep."

When God gets into the depths of our hearts, He purifies every intention of the thoughts and the joys. We are told in the Word it is joy unspeakable and full of glory.

Beloved, it is truth that the commandments were written on tables of stone. Moses, like a great big, loving father over Israel, had a heart full of joy because God had showed him a plan where Israel could be made to partake of great things through these commandments. But God says, "Not in tables of stone," which made the face of Moses to shine with great joy. Deeper than that, more wonderful than that: the commandments in our hearts; the deep love of God in our hearts, the deep movings of eternity rolling in and bringing God in. Hallelujah!

Oh, beloved, let God the Holy Ghost have His way today in so unfolding to us all the grandeurs of His glory.

TONGUES AND INTERPRETATION: "The Spirit, He Himself, it is He, that waketh thee morning by morning and unfolds unto thee in thy heart, tenderness, compassion and love towards thy Maker till thou dost weep before Him and say to Him, in the spirit, 'Thou art mine! Thou art mine!'"

Yes, He is mine! Beloved, He is mine!

"And such trust have we through Christ to God-ward:

"Not that we are sufficient of ourselves to think anything as of ourselves; but our sufficiency is of God." (vv. 4, 5).

Ah, it is lovely! Those verses are to keep to pass over. Beloved, that is a climax of divine exaltation that is so much different from human exaltation.

The end is not yet, praise the Lord!
The end is not yet, praise the Lord!
Your blessings He is bestowing,
And my cup is overflowing,
And the end is not yet, praise the Lord!

We want to get to a place where we are beyond trusting in ourselves. Beloved, there is so much failure in self-assurances. It is not bad to have good things on the lines of satisfaction, but we must never have anything on the human that we rest upon. There is only one sure place to rest upon, and our trust is in God.

In Thy name we go. In Thee we trust. And God brings us off in victory. When we have no confidence in ourselves to trust in ourselves but when our whole trust rests upon the authority of the mighty God, He has promised to be with us at all times, and to make the path straight, and to make all the mountains a way. Then we understand how it is that David could say, "Thy gentleness hath made me great."

Ah, thou lover of souls! We have no confidence in the flesh. Our confidence can only be stayed and relied in the One who never fails, in the One who knows the end from the beginning, in the One who is able to come in at the midnight hour as easy as in the noonday, and make the night and the day alike to the man who rests completely in the will of God, knowing that "all things work together tor good to them that love Him," and trust in Him. And such trust have we in Him.

This is the worthy position where God would have all souls to be. We should find that we would not run His errands and make mistakes; we would not be dropping down in the wrong place. We would find our life was as surely in the canon of thought with God as the leading of the children of Israel through the wilderness. And we should be able to say, Not one good thing hath the Lord withheld from me (Psalm 84 : 11), and "... all the promises of God in him are yea, and in him Amen, unto the glory of God by us" (2 Corinthians 1 : 20).

The Lord has helped me to have no confidence in myself, but to wholly trust in Him, bless His name!

Who also hath made us able ministers of the new testament; not of the letter, but of the spirit: for the letter killeth, but the spirit giveth life. But if the ministration of death, written and engraved in stones, was glorious, so that the children of Israel could not steadfastly behold the face of Moses for the glory of his countenance;

which glory was to be done away: How shall not the ministration of the spirit be rather glorious? For if the ministration of condemnation be glory, much more doth the ministration of righteousness exceed in glory. 2 Corinthians 3:6-9

Let us enter into these great words on the line of holy thoughtfulness. If I go on with God He wants me to understand all His deep things. He doesn't want anybody in the Pentecostal church to be novices, or to deal with the Word of God on natural grounds. We can understand the Word of God only by the Spirit of God.

We cannot define, or separate, or deeply investigate and unfold this holy plan of God without we have the life of God, the thought of God, the Spirit of God, and the revelation of God. The Word of Truth is pure, spiritual, and divine. If you try to divide it on natural grounds you will only finish up on natural lines for natural man, but you will never satisfy a Pentecostal Assembly.

The people who are spiritual can only be fed on spiritual material. So if you are expecting your messages to catch fire you will have to have them on fire. You won't have to light the message up in the meeting. You will have to bring the message red-hot, burning, living. The message must be direct from heaven. It must be as truly, "Thus saith the Lord," as the Scriptures which are, "Thus saith the Lord," because you will only speak as the Spirit gives utterance, and you will always be giving fresh revelation. You will never be stale on any line, whatever you say will be fruitful, elevating the mind, lifting the people, and all the people will want more.

To come into this we must see that we not only need the baptism of the Spirit but we need to come to a place where there is only the baptism of the Spirit left. Look at the first verse of the fourth chapter of Luke and you will catch this beautiful truth:

And Jesus being full of the Holy Ghost returned from Jordan, and was led by the Spirit into the wilderness.

But look at Mark 1: 12 and you will find He was driven of the Spirit into the wilderness:

And immediately the Spirit driveth him into the wilderness.

In John's gospel Jesus says He does not speak or act of Himself:

...the words that I speak unto you I speak not of myself: but the Father that dwelleth in me, he doeth the works. John 14:10

We must know that the baptism of the Spirit immerses us into an intensity of zeal, into a likeness to Jesus, to make us into pure, running metal so hot for God that it travels like oil from vessel to vessel. This divine line of the Spirit will let us see that we have ceased and we have begun. We are at the end for a beginning. We are down and out, and God is in and out.

There isn't a thing in the world can help us in this meeting. There isn't a natural thought that can be of any use here. There isn't a thing that is carnal, earthly, natural, that can ever live in these meetings. It must only have one pronouncement, it has to die eternally because there is no other plan for a baptized soul, only dead indeed.

God, help us to see then that we may be filled with the letter without being filled with the Spirit. We may be filled with knowledge without having divine knowledge. And we may be filled with wonderful things on natural lines and still remain a natural man. But you cannot do it in this truth that I am dealing with this morning. No man is able to walk this way without He is in the Spirit. He must live in the Spirit and he must realize all the time that he is growing in that same ideal of his Master, in season and out of season, always beholding the face of the Master, Jesus.

David says, "I foresaw the Lord for He was on my right hand that I should not be moved. Then my tongue was glad." Praise the Lord!

For even that which was made glorious had no glory in this respect, by reason of the glory that excelleth. For if that which is done away was glorious, much more that which remaineth is glorious. 2 Corinthians 3:10,11

I notice here that the one has to be done away, and the other has to increase. One day I was having a good time on this chapter. I had a lot of people before me who were living on the 39 Articles and Infant Baptism, and all kinds of things. The Lord showed me that all these things had to be done away. I find there is no place into all the further plan with God without you absolutely putting them to one side. "Done away."

Is it possible to do away with the commandments? Yes and no. If they are not so done away with you that you have no consciousness of keeping commandments, then they are not done away. If you know you are living holy, you don't know what holiness is. If you know you are keeping commandments, you don't know what keeping commandments is.

These things are done away. God has brought us in to be holy without knowing it, and keeping the whole truth without knowing it, living in it, moving in it, acting in it, a new creation in the Spirit. The old things are done away. If there is any trouble in you at all, it shows you have not come to the place where you are at rest.

"Done away." God, help us to see it. If the teaching is a bit too high for you, ask the Lord to open your eyes to come into it. For there is no man here has power in prayer, or has power in life with God if he is trying to keep the commandments. They are done away, brother. And thank God, the very doing away with them is fixing them deeper in our hearts than ever before. For out of the depths we cry unto God, and in the depths has He turned righteousness in, and uncleanness out. It is unto the depths we cry unto God in these things. May God lead us all every step of the way in His divine leading.

Ye are Our Epistle, part 2

A two part message given the same morning at Glad Tidings Tabernacle and Bible Training School, 1536, Ellis Street, San Francisco, California August 23, 1922

I am going to commence with the sixth verse of the third chapter of Second Corinthians, lest you stop in "the letter."

Who also hath made us able ministers of the new testament; not of the letter; but of the spirit: for the letter killeth, but the spirit giveth life. But if the ministration of death, written and engraven in stones, was glorious, so that the children of Israel could not steadfastly behold the face of Moses for the glory of his countenance; which glory was to be done away: How shall not the ministration of the spirit be rather glorious? For if the ministration of condemnation be glory, much more doth the ministration of righteousness exceed in glory. For even that which was made glorious had no glory in this respect, by reason of the glory that excelleth. For if that which is done away was glorious, much more that which remaineth is glorious. Seeing then that we have such hope, we use great plainness of speech: And not as Moses, which put a veil over his face, that the children of Israel could not steadfastly look to the end of that which is abolished: But their minds were blinded: for until this day remaineth the same veil untaken away in the reading of the old testament; which veil is done away in Christ. But even unto this day, when Moses is read, the veil is upon their heart. Nevertheless when it shall tum to the Lord, the veil shall be takm away. Now the Lord is that Spirit: and where the Spirit of the Lord is, there is liberty. But we all, with open face beholding as in a glass the glory of the Lord, are changed into the same image from glory to glory, even as by the Spirit of the Lord. 2 Corinthians 3:6-18

Think about that; even the glory that was on the face of Moses had to be done away for what reason? For something that had exceeding glory. I am positive we have no conception of the depths and heights of the liberties and blessings and incarnations of the Spirit. We must attain to these positions of godliness and we must be partakers of His divine nature. Praise the Lord!

How shall not the ministration of the spirit be rather glorious? For if the ministration of condemnation be glory, much more doth the ministration of righteousness exceed in glory. 2 Corinthians 3:8,9

The Lord help us now on this. I see the truth as it was brought to them in the law as we read last Sunday morning. Paul had something to glory in when he kept the law, and was blameless, but he said he threw that to one side to win Him which is greater even than that.

Now we come to the truth of this: what is there in the law that isn't glorious? Nothing. It was so glorious that Moses was filled with joy in the expectation of what it was. But what is ours in the excellence of glory? It is this, that we live, we move, we reign over all things and it isn't" Do, do, do." It is a "Will, will, will." And I rejoice to do. It is no more, Thou shalt not." It is a will. "I delight to do Thy will, O God!" So it is far exceeding in glory. And beloved, in our hearts there is exceeding glory. Oh, the joy of this celestial touch this morning!

TONGUES AND INTERPRETATION: "The living God who is chastening us after this manner, is always building us after His manner that there may be no spot in us. For the Lord Himself has designed the plan, and is working out in us His divine mind, and is taking the man and transforming him in this plan till he loses his identity in the mighty God of possibilities."

Hallelujah! We praise Thee, O God. And we will praise Him forever.

> Far above all,
> Far above all,
> God hath exalted Him,
> Far above all.

Amen! Glory to God! Thank God for that interpretation. I shall be glad to read that, I don't know what I said, only I know the joy of it.

Oh, yes, it exceeds in glory. It is an excellent glory. When Peter is rehearsing that wonderful day in the mount, he says, "There came such a voice to Him from the excellent glory." And so we are hearing this morning from the excellent glory. It is so lovely.

If I come along to you this morning and say, "Whatever you do, you must try to be holy," I should miss it. I should be altogether outside of this plan. But I take the words of the epistle this morning by the Holy Ghost that says, "Be ye holy."

It is as easy as possible to be holy, but you can never be holy by trying to be. But when you lose your heart and another takes your heart, and you lose your desires and He takes the desires, then you live in that sunshine of bliss which no mortal can ever touch.

Divine immortality swallows up all natural mortality. And God wants us to see that we have to be entirely eaten up by this holy zeal of God so that every day we walk in the Spirit. It is lovely to walk in the Spirit, then ye shall not fulfill any part of the law but the Spirit will cause you to dwell in safety and rejoice inwardly, and praise God reverently, and make you know that you are an increasing force of immortality swallowing up life. Hallelujah!

Ah, it is lovely! I will never be cross anymore.

Beloved, it is impossible to go on with God and have the old life jumping up. Glory to God!

For if the ministration of condemnation be glory, much more doth the ministration of righteousness exceed in glory. 2 Corinthians 3 : 9

This is a beautiful word. I want to speak about "righteousness" now. There is nothing so beautiful as righteousness. You cannot touch these beatitudes we are dwelling on this morning without seeing the excellent glory exists right in the Christ. All the excellent glory is in Him. All righteousness is in Him.

Everything that pertains to holiness, and godliness, everything that denounces and brings to death the natural, everything that makes you know you have ceased to be forever, is always in the knowledge of an endless power of a risen Christ.

I want you to notice there is an excellent glory about it. Whenever you look at Jesus you can look at so many different facts of His life. I see Him in those forty days, with wonderful truth, infallible proof of His ministry. What was the ministry of Christ? When you come to the very essence of His ministry it was the righteousness of His purpose. The excellence of His ministry was the glory that covered Him. His Word was convincing, inflexible, divine with a personality of an eternal endurance. It never failed.

The righteousness of God. If He said it, it was there. He said it and it stood fast. It was an immutable condition with Him. When God spoke it was done. And His righteousness abideth. God must have us there. We must be people of our word. People ought to be able to depend upon our word.

If there were only five saved in a meeting we should never say there were six. If there were five baptized we should never say there were seven. If the building would hold 500 people we should never say it was packed and had a thousand in it. He is establishing righteousness in our hearts that we shall not exaggerate on any line.

Jesus was true inwardly and outwardly. He is the way, the truth and the life, and on these things we can build; on these things we can pray; on these things we can live. When we know that our own heart condemneth us not, we can say to the mountain, "Be removed." But when our own hearts condemn us, there is no power in prayer, no power in preaching, or in anything. We are just sounding brass and tinkling cymbals.

May God the Holy Ghost show us there must be a ministry of righteousness. We ought to stand by our signature, and abide by it. And if we were cut through they would find pure gold right through us. That is what I call righteousness. He was righteousness through and through. He is lovely! Oh, truly, He is beautiful!

One thing God wants to fix in our hearts is to be like Him. Be like Him in character. Don't be troubled so much about your faces but be more concerned about your hearts. All the powder won't change the heart. All the adorning of silks and satins won't make purity. Beloved, if I was going down a road and I saw a fox tail sticking out of a hole I shouldn't ask anybody what there was inside. And if there is anything hanging outside, you know what there is inside. Righteousness in the inward parts. Pure through and through.

Hearken! There is an excellent glory attached to it. We read:

For if the ministration of condemnation be glory, much more doth the ministration of righteousness exceed in glory. 2 Corinthians 3:9

The Bible is the plumbline of everything. And without we are plumbed right up with the Word of God, we will fail in the measure in which we are not righteous. And so may God the Holy Ghost bring us, this morning, into that blessed ministry of righteousness. Amen! Glory to God!

For even that which was made glorious had no glory in this respect, by reason of the glory that excelleth. 2 Corinthians 3 : 10

Come again right to the law. I see that it was truly a schoolmaster that brought us to Christ. I like the thought of it, that law is beautiful, law is established in the earth. As far as possible in every country and town, you will find the law has something to do with keeping things straight. And in a measure the city has some kind of sobriety because of the law.

But beloved, we are belonging to a higher, to a nobler citizenship, and it isn't an earthly citizenship, for our citizenship is in heaven. So we must see thee is an excellent glory about this position we are holding this morning. For if the natural law will keep an earthly city in somewhat moderate conditions, what will the excellent glory be in the divine relationship of the citizenship to which we belong?

What I mean by excellent glory, it outshines. It makes all the people feel a longing to go. What there is about the excellent glory is this: the earth is filled with broken hearts, but the excellent glory is filled with redeemed men and women, filled with the excellency of the graces of the glory of God. Oh, glorious is the excellent glory! Ah, praise the Lord, oh my soul! Hallelujah!

For if that which is done away was glorious, much more that which remaineth is glorious. Seeing then that we have such hope, we use great plainness of speech: And not as Moses, which put a veil over his face, that the children of Israel could not steadfastly look to the end of that which is abolished. 2 Corinthians 3:11-13

Yesterday morning I was preaching to preachers, but we can see that this message is for the perfecting of preachers. The man who is going on with God will have no mix-up in his oratory. He will be so plain and precise, and divine in his leadings, that everything will have a lift towards the glory. And you will always realize he will not play about to satisfy human curiosity. He must have his mind upon higher things altogether, and he must see God would not have him loiter about. He must "use great plainness of speech." He must be a man who knows his message. He must know what God has in His mind in the Spirit, not in the letter, because no man that is going to speak by the Spirit of God knows what God is going to say in the meeting.

He is there a vessel for honor, His mouthpiece, and all contained there is of God. And therefore, he stands in the presence of God, and God speaks and uses him. But hearken! God is a Spirit working within the human life with thought, with might, with truth and life, and brings out of the great treasury of His mightiness into the human life, into the heart, and sends it right through onto the canvas of the mind, and the language comes out according to the operation of the Spirit of God.

Beloved, shall we any more try any lines but the divine? Every man is not just in the same order, but I could say to the man with faith that there is a touch of faith for that man to come into as a spiritual orator. He has to forget all he has put on his notes because of a higher order of notes.

I always say you cannot sing victory on a minor key. And you never can have a spiritual horizon on a low note. If your life isn't constant pitch, you will never ring the bells of heaven. You must always be in tune with God, and then the music will come out as sweet as possible.

Let us get away from going into libraries and filling our minds with human theology. Not that I want to discourage anybody, but it would pay the best man here, I don't care who he is, to go home and set fire to his library. You say that is a silly thing? I would not have said it if I had not the best thing to put into it after it is burned down. I don't say, Go home and do it straightway. Think over it first. The more you think over it the more you will want to burn it.

I am not here for any other purpose than for the glory of God. God forbid! I have known so many people who have been barren and helpless, and they have used other people's material on the platform. If you ever turn to another man's material you have dropped from the higher sense of an orator from heaven.

We must now be the mouthpiece of God, not by letter but by the Spirit. And we must be so in the will of God that God rejoices over us with singing. Isn't it lovely? We are going forward a little. Let us turn now to the thirteenth and fourteenth verses:

And not as Moses, which put a veil over his face, that the children of Israel could not steadfastly look to the end of that which is abolished:

But their minds were blinded: for until this day remaineth the same veil untaken away in the reading of the old testament; which veil is done away in Christ. 2 Corinthians 3:13,14

I have nothing to say about the Jew except this: that I know I am saved by the blood of a Jew. I owe my Bible to the Jews, for the Jews have kept it for us. We have a Savior who was a Jew. The first proclamation of the Gospel was of the Jews. I know that I owe everything to the Jew today, but I see that the Jew will never have the key to unlock the Scriptures till he sees Jesus. The moment he does he will see this truth that Jesus gave to Peter:

And I say also unto thee, That thou art Peter, and upon this rock I will build my church...And I will give unto thee the keys of the kingdom of heaven. Matthew 16:18,19

And I will give thee the key of truth, the key to unveil. The key was brought in the moment Peter saw the Lord. The moment they see Christ, the whole of the Scriptures is opened out to the Jew. That will be a great day when the Jews see the Lord. They will see Him!

But their minds were blinded: for until this day remaineth the same veil untaken away in the reading of the old testament; which veil is done away in Christ.

But even unto this day, when Moses is read, the veil is upon their heart. 2 Corinthians 3:14,15

God doesn't say the veil is upon their mind, but upon their heart. And beloved, God can never save a man through his mind. He saves him through his heart. He can never bring all the glories into a man's life by his mind. He must touch the deep things of his heart.

Nevertheless when it shall turn to the Lord, the veil shall be taken away. Now the Lord is that Spirit: and where the Spirit of the Lord is, there is liberty. But we all, with open face beholding as in a glass the glory of the Lord, are changed into the same image from glory to glory, even as by the Spirit of the Lord. 2 Corinthians 3:16-18

I must speak about liberty first. There are two kinds of liberty, two kinds of grace. We must never use liberty but we must be in the place where liberty can use us. If we use liberty we shall be as dead as possible, and it will all end up in a fizzle.

But if we are in the Spirit, the Lord of life is the same Spirit. I believe it is right to jump for joy but don't jump till the joy makes you jump because if you do you will jump flat. If you jump as the joy makes you jump you will bounce up again.

In the Spirit I know there is any amount of divine plan. If the Pentecostal people had only come into it in meekness and in the true knowledge of God, it would all be so manifest that every heart in the meeting would be moved by that Spirit.

Now the Lord is that Spirit: and where the Spirit of the Lord is, there is liberty. 2 Corinthians 3:17

Liberty has a thousand sides to it, but there is no liberty which is going to help the people so much as testimony. I find people who don't know how to testify right. We must testify only as the Spirit gives utterance. We find in Revelation that the testimony of Jesus is the spirit of prophecy.

When your flesh is keeping you down, but your heart is so full it is lifting you up - have you ever been like that? The flesh has been fastening you to the seat but your heart has been bubbling over. At last the heart has had more power and you have risen up.

And then in that heart affection for Jesus in the Spirit of love and in the knowledge of truth, you begin to testify, and when you have done you sit down. Liberty used wrongly goes on when you finished and spoils the meeting. You are not to use your liberty except for the glory of God.

So many churches are spoiled by long prayers, and long testimonies. The speaker can tell, if he keeps in the Spirit, when he should sit down. When you begin to rehearse yourself, the people get wearied and tired and they wish you would sit down. The unction ceases, they sit down worse than when they rose up.

It is nice for a man to begin cold, and warm up as he goes on. When he catches fire and sits down in the midst of it he will keep the fire afterwards. Look! It is lovely to pray, and it is a joy to hear you pray, but when you go on after you are done, all the people are tired of it.

So God wants us to know that we are not to use liberty because we have it to use, but we are to let the liberty use us, and we should know when to end.

This excellent glory should go on to a liberality to everybody, and this would prove that all the Church is in liberty. The Church ought to be free so that the people always go away feeling, "Oh, I wish the meeting bad gone on for another hour." Or, "What a glorious time we had at that prayer meeting!" Or, "Wasn't that testimony meeting a revelation!" That is the way to finish up. Never finish up with something too long, finish up with something too short. Then everybody comes again to piece up where they left off.

The last verse is the most glorious of all for us:

But we all, with open face beholding as in a glass the glory of the Lord, are changed into the same image from glory to glory, even as by the Spirit of the Lord. 2 Corinthians 3:18

So there are glories upon glories, and joys upon joys, exceeding joyous and abundance of joys, and a measureless measure of all the lot. Beloved, we get the word so wonderfully in our hearts that it absolutely changes us in everything. And we so feast on the Word of the Lord, so eat and digest the truth, so inwardly eat of Him, till we are absolutely changed every day from one state to another.

As we look into the perfect mirror of the face of the Lord we are changed from one state of grace to another, from glory to glory. You will never find anything else but the Word of God that takes you there. So you cannot afford to put aside that Word.

I beseech you, beloved, that you come short of none of these beatitudes w have been speaking of, in your life. These grand truths of the Word of God must be your testimony, must be your life, your pattern. You must be in it, in fact you are of it. "Ye are...the epistle of Christ," God says to you by the Spirit. Then let us see that we put off everything that by the grace of God we may put on everything.

Where there is a standard which hasn't been reached in your life, God in His grace, by His mercy and your yieldedness, can fit you for that place that you can never be prepared for only by a broken heart and a contrite spirit, yielding to the will of God. If you will come with a whole heart to the throne of grace, God will meet you and build you on His spiritual plane. Amen. Praise the Lord!

Great Grace Upon the Church

Preached at Pentecostal Union Meeting, Chicago October 31, 1922

And great grace was upon them all." Great grace is upon us when we magnify the Lord. If ever you want to see what God means when He gets a chance at His people, have a peep at the fourth chapter of Acts, and see what God did. Just because all the people shouted aloud to Him He imparted to them such blessing that every person was filled with the Holy Ghost, and I believe what God wants to do in these days is to give an inward manifestation of His divine presence within the body until the body is moved by the power of the Spirit. Beloved, we are accustomed to earthly things, but when God sends the heavenly it is beyond our understanding. Oh, to have the revelation of the mind of God! It fills my soul, the thought of it ! Oh, for the kind of loosening of the body that we will never be bound again! Just filled with God!

I believe God wants us to understand something of the words of this life. What life? The manifestation of the power of Jesus in the human body, a divine life, a divine power, a quickening, thrilling energy given to you. I was baptized with the Holy Ghost in 1907. If anyone had said to me: "Now, Wigglesworth, you will see such and such things," it would have been beyond my human comprehension, but the tide has risen for fifteen years, and it is still rising. Thank God, there has never been a black day, nor a blank day.

When I think about the first Church, how God favored her, how He burst thru her, how He definitely spoke, how He transformed Christians and made them move with the power of apostles, that wherever they went they transformed lives-God did such wonderful things, and when I think of it, I think, that we should have something far in advance, and say: "Look up; your redemption draweth nigh!" I want to take a perspective of what they were, and we must be. I am inwardly convinced of the power that awaits us, the installation of God's movement right in our hearts.

I notice in the first Church it wasn't possible for a lie to live, and I want you to keep in mind that there is a time coming when nothing of uncleanness will be able to remain in His little flock. The first Church was so pure God overshadowed it; He nursed it, brought it thru, and He has His hand upon us at this time. How do we know? The Lord hath laid the foundation which is an immovable foundation. It is built upon the prophets; it is built upon the apostles; it is built upon the Word of God, and the church will yet come into the fullness of the manifestation of the body of Christ.

God will keep His Word. The church will be ready like a bride adorned for her husband; the gifts will be a ministry clothed upon; the graces will adorn the believer, and will be far beyond anything we have seen.

Now, Ananias and Sapphira were, I believe, baptized believers. I have a firm conviction in my heart that God in the first outpouring of the Spirit did His work so beautifully that those three thousand who were pricked in their hearts met the condition of the Bible pattern. Peter said unto them: "Repent, believe, be baptized and ye shall receive the gift of the Holy Ghost." They obeyed and we have reason to believe they received the Holy Ghost. I cannot conceive of anything else but what the Early Church all received the outpouring of the Holy Ghost. And I believe today that we should press home to every soul the necessity of meeting the conditions and being filled with the Holy Ghost. Then I notice here in this fifth chapter of Acts that God had the particular oversight of the Church. I love to think of this. They gave of their substance, they gave willingly; they laid it down at the apostles' feet, and they were so eager to give that they began selling their property, and brought the proceeds to the apostles. Now there were two people who had sold the land who began to talk over the thing at home, and this was the sense of their argument: "This thing may go down; it may leak out. If we give it all, we shall lose it all and have nothing left," and so they reserved for themselves a portion, but they missed it. Listen: God never wants anything from you but a spontaneous heart gift, and anyone who gives spontaneously to God will always get a big cup full. God is never in any man's debt.

I notice the moment God visited this people in showing up this sin and bringing death to Ananias and Sapphira, it instantly brought a tremendous fear over all the church, a fear that brought an answer. There is a fear that brings an answer. Were they afraid of God? No, it was something better than that. When they saw that God was there in judgment upon them they turned with a holy fear, with a reverence. It sobered things and the people began to see that God was zealous for them. There are two kinds of fear, one that is afraid of God, and another fear that loves God, and that was the fear that came over them, the fear of grieving God, which the Lord wants us to have. Oh, to fear Him in such a way that you would rather be shot than to grieve Him! That is it. This came over the people, and when it came, another thing happened. "No one durst join themselves to them." That was a wonderful time. May God so sanctify His church that no one durst come near without he means business. Brother, did God have a hand in your plan? Did you join this people because you felt they were a choice people, or did you have the constraining power of God upon you?

I see more and more in this glorious life of God, that there is a pure whiteness to be achieved, there is a pure sonship without fear and the saints of God shall rise in such confidence until they will remove what people think are mountains, till they will subdue what you call kingdoms.

I have had some wonderful times in Belfast, and in fact all over Ireland. I was in Belfast one day and a young man came to me and said: "Brother Wigglesworth, I am very much distressed," and he told me why. They had an old lady in their assembly who used to pray heaven down upon them. She had an accident. Her thigh was broken and they took her away to the infirmary. They put her in a plaster of Paris cast and she was in that condition for five months. Then they broke the cast and lifted her on to her feet and asked her to walk. She fell again and broke her leg in another place. And they found out that the first break had never knit together. They brought her home and laid heron the couch and the young man asked me to go and pray for her. When I got into the house I asked: "Do you believe that God can heal you?" She said "Yes. When I heard you had come to the city I thought, 'This is my chance to be healed.' "An old man, her husband, was sitting in a chair, had been sitting there for four years; helpless. And he said: "I do not believe. I will not believe. She was the only help I had. She has been taken away with a broken leg, and they have brought her back with her leg broken twice. How can I believe God?"

I turned to her and said: "Now is it all right?" "Yes," she said, "it is all right." The right leg was broken in two parts. Physicians can join up bones beautifully, and make them fit together, but if God doesn't come in with His healing power, there is no physician can heal them. As soon as the oil was placed upon her head and hands laid on, instantly down the right limb there was a stream of life, and she knew it. She said: "I am healed." I said: "If you are healed, you do not need anybody to help you." J went out. She took hold of the mantle shelf above her head and pulled herself up and walked all around the room. She was perfectly healed.

The old man said: "Make me walk." I said: "You old sinner, repent." Then he began: "You know, Lord, I didn't mean it." I really believe he was in earnest, and to show you the mercy and compassion of God, the moment I laid hands upon him, the power of God went thru him and he rose up after four years being stiff and walked around the room. That day both he and his wife were made whole. Do you not believe now that God has a plan in all these things? I want you to realize that what God wants to do in us and thru us in these days is to blend us together, give us one heart and one mind. They were all of one heart and one mind, and they had such faith that the shadow of Peter worked a transformation in their bodies. Of course, it was God that did the healing. But as Peter came along I can see the people moved by his presence. Beloved, we have one in the meeting tonight who is a million times mightier than Peter. His touch will set you free. It is the living virtue! "Go speak to the people the words of this life," the life of the Son of God, the quickener by the Word.

The first outpouring was of the Spirit, and the latter is to be the fullness of the Spirit. When God's mighty power shakes the foundation and purifies, there is a transformation. The Lord is the life, and where the life of the Spirit and the Word are together they bring forth an issue of transforming and quickening until the man is made like Jesus. Jesus is the first fruits. It is lovely to think that God sent Him in the likeness of sinful flesh, and for sin condemned sin in the flesh. Then we are here tonight with a clear conception of this thing, that the life of Jesus has come into our flesh and delivered us from the power of darkness and disease, from bitterness and covetousness, idolatry and lust; from the corruption of the present evil world, by the same Spirit, the same life.

I believe the Lord would have me take you to a moment in my life. I was having some meetings in Belfast, and this is the rising tide of what I believe was the move of the Spirit in a certain direction, to show the greatness of that which was to follow. Night after night the Lord had led me on certain lines of truth. There was so much in it that one felt they could not give up, and every night until ten o'clock we were opening up the Word of God. They came to me and said: "Brother, we have been feasting and are so full we are ready for a burst of some kind. Don't you think it is time to call an altar service?" I said I knew that God was working and the time would come when the altar service would be called, but we would have to get the mind of the Lord upon it. There was nothing more said. They began early in the afternoon to bring the sick people. We never had a thing said about it. The meeting came and every seat was taken up, the window sills were filled and every nook and corner. The glory of God filled the place. It was the easiest thing in the world to preach; it came forth like a river, and the power of God rested mightily. There were a lot of people who had been seeking the baptism for years. Sinners were in the meeting, and a number of sick people. What happened? God hears me say this: There was a certain moment in that meeting when every sick person was healed, every lame person was healed, and every sinner saved, and it all took place in five minutes. There comes into a meeting sometimes something we cannot understand, and it is amazing how things happen.

When I was on the ship there was a man who had trained all his life, as it were, to be a physician. He got to be eminent and was looked up to as one of the leading physicians, an Indian. He had been over to England to lecture, and was going back on the ship on which I was traveling. When the Christian Science lady got healed she saw the captain and told him what God had done. The Captain arranged a meeting and I had a fine chance to preach to all on the ship. The Indian doctor was there and he was struck with what happened. At the close of the meeting people decided for Christ; some people followed me into my stateroom, where God healed them. This Indian doctor came to me. "I am done," he said. "I have no spirit left. You must talk to me." For two hours we talked and God dealt with him. He stood before me. "I will never have any more medicine," he said. "God has saved me." That physician saw the power of God and recognized it. You ask, What is that? That is where God plans a life in a moment, thru one act. God wants the way into our lives. He wants to transform you by His grace. He wants to make you know that you are only here to be filled with His power and His presence for His glory. The "seed of the woman" must "bruise the serpent's head."

Now, beloved, the Acts of the Apostles were written to prove to us that the power and manifestation of God were to be continuous. Have you read about the scattering of these people at Jerusalem, how God was with them? Do not be afraid of persecution. I am never at my best until I am in a conflict, and until I have a fight with the enemy. They think I am rather unmerciful in my dealing with the sick, but I have no mercy for the devil and get him out at any cost. I resist him with all the power that is within me. God wrought mightily thru the persecution which came upon the church, and He could do the same today under similar circumstances.

Greater Works Than These

Address given at Colombo, Ceylon. 1926

I want all you people to have a good time, all to be at ease, all to be without pain, I want all to be free.

There is a man here with great pain in his head, I am going to lay my hands on him in the name of Jesus and he shall tell you what God has done, I believe that would be the right thing to do, before I begin to preach to you, to help this poor man so that he shall enjoy the meeting like us, without any pain.

(The man referred to was in pain with his head wrapped up in a bandage, and after be was prayed for testified that he had no pain.)

I want you all to be in a place where we receive much blessing from God. It is not possible for any of you to go out with pain, if you would only believe God, the Word of God if you receive it tonight, it is life, it gives deliverance to every captive. I want to preach the Word tonight so that all the people will know, you will go with a knowledge of the deliverance of God.

I want everyone to receive a blessing at the commencement of the meeting, no one person need to live out of the plan of God. If you have pain in your knee if you believe when you stand up as sure as you are there you will be free. I believe the Word of God. God has promised if we will believe we can have whatsoever we ask.

We want you to have it changed. The present tense tunes are better than future tense tunes. If you get a full salvation you will have a present tense tune. It is a good thing to be able to hope for sometimes... but it is a better thing to have it.

I used to hope and trust I would be baptized in the Holy Ghost, but, when I spoke in Tongues, no! when He spoke, then I knew I was baptized. Before, I used to hope it would be so. You cannot move a fact by an argument, when you get baptized in the Holy Ghost the Spirit speaks through you, then you know it is done- You Know the Comforter has come. Has He come to you? Has the Comforter come to you?

You must have Him, you must be filled with the Spirit, you must have an over- flowing, because Jesus says, after you have received the Holy Ghost ye shall have Power. We want you to have power.

Let us look at the Scriptures. Verily, verily I say that whatsoever you ask the Father in my name, I will do it, that the Father may be glorified in the Son. If ye shall ask anything in my name I will do it – I WILL DO IT, who says it? JESUS, that blessed Jesus, that lovely Jesus, that incarnation from heaven, that blessed Son of God. How He wants to bless, how He saves to the uttermost, no one spoke like He spoke. How ? Come unto me all ye that are weary and heavy laden and I will give you rest. Hear what Jesus says - I come not into the world to condemn the world, but that the world through me might be saved. How beautiful. Jesus wants us alt to be saved. Did you ever look at Him in His sympathy. Just take a vision of Him on Mount Olives and looking over Jerusalem weeping and saying Oh Jerusalem, Oh Jerusalem how often would I have gathered thee, and you would not. Shall it not be said of the people in Colombo, in Ceylon. How often would I have gathered thee as a hen gathered the chickens under her wings, and you would not. Will you. Hear what He said. WHATSOEVER YE SHALL ASK IN MY NAME I WILL DO IT. What do you want, how much do you want, do you want anything. Are you thirsty, are you hungry, Come unto me all that thirst and I will give you water of life, Are you hungry, he that eateth the flesh and drinketh the blood of the Son of man shall live forever.

Do you want to live forever. Jesus who saves to the uttermost, He heals, He helps all that come to Him.

How many are coming for healing? How many for salvation? Listen - Whatsoever ye ask in my name I will do it, the Word of the living God, The Son of God. How beautifully God speaks of Him - This is my beloved Son, and yet He gave Himself for us, He gave Himself as ransom for us, Amen.

How many are going to receive Him? Take the Water of Life freely. You may say, how can I take Him. Believe on the Lord Jesus Christ and you shall be saved. What is it to believe. He that heareth my Word and believeth on Him that sent me hath everlasting life.

Who are the people that followed Jesus – they that love Him in their hearts. Do you love Him in your hearts. From this day if you do love Him you will begin to hate all kinds of sin and you will love all kinds of righteousness, that is the secret. The man that says he loves God and loves the world – he is a liar. God says the truth is not in him. If a man loves the world the love of the Father is not in him, and you can tell tonight whether you love God or not. Do you love the world, then the love of the father is not in you. If you hate the world, then the love of the Lord Jesus is in you. Hallelujah.

I want to make you love Him. Is He worth loving? What has He done? He bought salvation, He died to deliver, The wages of sin is death. The gift of God is eternal life.

I leave it with you. will you love Him, will you serve Him. Will you. He knows it He understands.

> There's no one that loves me like Jesus,
> There's no one that knows me like Him,
> Be knows all your sickness He knows all your sickness
> There's no one that knows me like Him.

That's what He says. COME UNTO ME. He knows you are needy.

I want you to be blessed now, I find I get blessed as I ask, in the street, everywhere. If you find me in the street or anywhere, if I am alone I shall be talking to God, I make it my business to talk to God all the time If I wake in the night I make it my business to pray and that's the reason I believe that God keeps me right, always right, always ready. I believe that God the Holy Ghost keeps us living in communion with God.

I want you to begin now, begin talking to God.

PRAYER.

John 14:12.

Jesus was the way and the truth, and therefore all that Jesus said was true. Jesus said truly, truly, if you believe greater works than these shall ye do because I go to the father. Has He gone? If I told you earthly things and left them - now I tell you heavenly things. The son of man is down, the son of man is up. The greatest and one of the deepest truths possible for the believer.

Do you see this Electric Light. That light is receiving power from the dynamo, it has a receiver and transmitter. The power house may be a mile or two away, the wires that are conveying the current to and from are covered. Where you are getting the light is bare wire, the juice is passing through the bare wire and gives you the light.

To bring it to you to night to understand the life in Christ. Jesus sends the light, and life through, and it illuminates the life then returns and just as you are holy inside, the revelation of God is made manifest and the life becomes full of illumination. My life is from Him, my life receives back to Him, and I am kept by the life of God.

I touch them and instantly they change. The Life of the Son of God goes through and passes on. I live by the faith of the Son of God.

He that believeth on Me - he that believeth. The devils believe and tremble. People follow Scripture as if it had nothing to do with it. The Scripture may be Life or letter. My spirit - my Word - what is the Word. It is spirit and life giving when we believe. What is believing, Believing is the asking of the divine life that God gives to Him. Who desires. Everyone in this place can have Divine Life.

We do not believe in baptismal regeneration. You cannot be saved by riches. Jesus says ye must be born again... The new birth comes through faith in the Lord Jesus Christ, and you can be saved in the field as well as in a church. It is the heart, when the heart desires after righteousness, God makes Himself known, so we want you to be saved by the Blood tonight. Someone says I want to be saved.. Shall I bring you to the Word, he that asketh receiveth, who says - Jesus says, he that asks receives.

> If I ask Him to receive me
> Will He say me nay,
> Not till earth and not till heaven
> Pass away.

Salvation is of the Lord. No man can save you, no man can heal you. If anyone has been healed in these meetings it is the Lord that has healed them.

I would not take it under any circumstances that I can heal anybody, but I believe His Word - He that believeth on me greater works than these shall he do because I go to my Father. He is lovely, Lovely Jesus.

> He knows it all, He knows it all,
> My Father knows it all,
> The bitter tears how fast they fall,
> He knows, my Father knows it all.

Is not He lovely, if You get saved tonight you will have another song

> He knows it all, He knows it all,
> My father knows it all
> The joy that comes that overflows
> He knows, my Father knows it all.

Before I was baptized in the Holy Ghost, there were many songs I used to sing as they were written. God began a change; and He changed many songs. I believe God wants to change the Song in your heart.

>   He changed this song for me.
>   This is how it is sung,
>   Oh then it will be glory for me
>   It will be glory for me.
>   But God changed it,
>   Oh it is now Glory for me.
>   It is now glory for me,
>   As now by His grace I can look on His face,
>   Now it is glory, Glory for me.

Like Precious Faith, part 1

Sermon preached at Glad Tidings Tabernacle and Bible Training School, 1536, Ellis Street, San Francisco, California August 1, 1922

God will do great things for us if we are prepared to receive them from Him. We are dull of comprehension because we let the cares of this world blind our eyes, but if we keep open to God, He has a greater plan for us in the future than we have seen or ever have dreamed about in the past. It is God's delight to fulfill to us impossibilities because of His omnipotence, and when we reach the place where He alone has the right of way in all things, then all mists and misunderstandings will clear away.

I have been asking the Lord for His message for you this morning, and I believe He would have me turn to the second epistle of Peter, first chapter, beginning with the first verse:

Simon Peter, a servant and an apostle of Jesus Christ, to them that have obtained like precious faith with us through the righteousness of God and our Savior Jesus Christ: Grace and peace be multiplied unto you through the knowledge of God, and of Jesus our Lord, According as his divine power hath given unto us all things that pertain unto life and godliness, through the knowledge of him that hath called us to glory and virtue: Whereby are given unto us exceeding great and precious promises: that by these ye might be partakers of the divine nature, having escaped the corruption that is in the world through lust. And beside this, giving all diligence, add to your faith virtue; and to virtue knowledge; and to knowledge temperance; and to temperance patience; and to patience godliness; And to godliness brotherly kindness; and to brotherly kindness charity. For if these things be in you, and abound, they make you that ye shall neither be barren nor unfruitful in the knowledge of our Lord Jesus Christ. Verses 1-8

Probably there is not a greater word that anyone could bring to an audience than this word, "like precious faith." "Like Precious Faith" means that God, who is from everlasting to everlasting, has always had people that He could trust; that He could illuminate, that He could enlarge until there was nothing within them that would hinder the power of God. Now this "Like Precious Faith" is the gift that God is willing to impart to all of us. He wants us to have this faith in order that we may "subdue kingdoms," "work righteousness," and, if it should be necessary, "stop the mouths of lions" (Hebrews 11:33).

We should be able under all circumstances to triumph. Not that we have any help in ourselves, but our help comes only from God, and if our help is only in God then we are always strong and never weak. It is always those people who are full of faith who have a "good report," who never murmur, who are in the place of victory, who are not in the place of human order, but of divine order in God. He is the Author of our faith, and our faith is always based on "thus saith the Lord."

This "Like Precious Faith" is for all. There is a word in the third chapter of Ephesians which is very good for us to consider: that you "may be able to comprehend with all saints..." (Ephesians 3:18). What does this "Like Precious Faith" mean to you this morning? Everyone here is receiving a blessing because of the faith of Abraham. But remember this, this "Like Precious Faith" is the same that Abraham had. This "Like Precious Faith" is the substance of the power of eternal life which is given to us through the Word. You may not be able to use this faith because of some hindrance in your life. I have had a thousand road engines come over my life to break me up and bring me to the place where this faith could operate within me. There is no way into the deep things of God, only through a broken spirit. When we are thus broken, we cease forever from our own works for Another, even Christ, has taken the reign. Faith in God, and power with God, come to us through the knowledge of the Word of God. Whatever we may think about it, it is true that we are no better than our faith. Whatever your estimation is of your own ability, of your own righteousness, or of your work in any way, you are no better than your faith.

How wonderful is this faith that overcomes the world! "He that believeth that Jesus is the Son of God overcomes the world!" But how does he overcome the world? If you believe in Him you are purified as He is pure. You are strengthened because He is strong. You are made whole because He is whole. All of His fullness may come into you because of the revelation of Himself. Faith is the living principle of the Word of God. If we yield ourselves up to be led by the Holy Spirit we shall be divinely led into the deep things of God, and the truths and revelations and all His mind will be made so clear unto us that we shall live by faith in Christ.

God has no thought of anything on a small scale. In the passage which we have read this morning are these words, "Grace and peace be 'multiplied' unto you through the knowledge of God, and of Jesus our Lord" (2 Peter 1:2). God's Word is always on the line of multiplication, and so I believe the Lord wants us on that line this morning. We see "Like Precious Faith" is to be obtained "through the righteousness of God and our Savior Jesus Christ." God's Word is without change. We are to be filled with the righteousness of God on the authority of the Word. His righteousness is from everlasting to everlasting, the same, yesterday and today and forever.

If I limit the Lord, He cannot work within me, but if I open myself to God then He will surely fill me and flow through me.

We must have this "Like Precious Faith" in order to have our prayers answered. If we ask anything according to God's will, we are told that He hears us, and if we know that He hears us, then we know we have the petitions that we desire. Oh, brothers, sisters, we must go into the presence of God and get from Him the answer to our prayers. Hear what Mark 11:24 says,

...What things soever ye desire, when ye pray, believe that ye receive them, and ye shall have them.

In the twenty-third verse we see mountains removed, difficulties all cleared away. When? When the man believes in his heart and refuses to doubt. We must have the reality, we must know God, we must be able to go into His presence and converse with God.

This "Like Precious Faith" goes on multiplying in grace and in peace through the knowledge of God. It places our feet on the Rock, and brings us to an unlimited place in our faith. This faith makes you dare to do anything with and for God. Remember that you can only be built up on the Word of God. If you build yourself on imagination or your own thoughts you will go wrong.

The Bible is the Word of God: supernatural in origin, eternal in duration, inexpressible in valor, infinite in scope, regenerative in power, infallible in authority, universal in interest, personal in application, inspired in totality. Read it through, write it down, pray it in, work it out, and then pass it on. Truly it is the Word of God. It brings into man the personality of God; it changes the man until he becomes the epistle of God. It transforms his mind, changes his character, takes him on from grace to grace, and gives him an inheritance in the Spirit. God comes in, dwells in, walks in, talks through, and sups with him.

Your peace be multiplied! You are to rejoice greatly. Oh! the bride ought to rejoice to hear the Bridegroom's voice. How we love our

Bridegroom and how He loves us! How adorable He is and how sweet is His countenance. At the presence of Jesus, all else goes.

Oh, my brother, my sister, we have the greatest tide of all our life. There is no tide like the power of the "latter rain." We must not fail to see what remarkable things God has for every one of us.

Beloved, I would like to press into your heart this morning the truth that God has no room for an ordinary man. God wants to take the ordinary man and put him through the sieve and bring him out into a place of extraordinary faith. The cry of our souls can be satisfied only with God. The great plan of God is to satisfy, you, and then give you the vision of something higher.

If ever you stop at any point, pick up at the place where you failed, and begin again under the refining light, and power and zeal of heaven and all things will be brought to you, for He will condescend to meet you.

Remember, beloved, it is not what you are but what God wants you to be. What shall we do? Shall we not dedicate ourselves afresh to God? Every new revelation brings a new dedication.

Let us seek Him.

Like Precious Faith, part 2

Published in Pentecostal Evangel p. 2-3 May 13, 1933

What would happen to us and to the needy world if we should get to the place where we really believed God? May God give us the desire to get to this place. Faith is a tremendous power, an inward mover. I am convinced that we have not yet seen all that God has for us, but if we shall only move on in faith we shall see the greater works.

When I was a little boy I remember asking my father for a pennyworth of something or other. He did not give it to me, so I sat down by his side and every now and again I would just quietly say, "Father!" He would appear to take no notice of me, but now and again I would touch him ever so gently and say, "Father!" My mother said to him, "Why don't you answer the child?" My father replied, "I have done so, but he won't accept my answer." Still I sat on, and occasionally I would touch him and say ever so quietly, "Father!" If he went out into the garden I followed him and occasionally I would touch his sleeve and say, "Father! Father! "Do you think I ever went away without the accomplishment of my desire? No, not once.

We need the same importunity as we go to God. We have the blessed assurance that if we ask anything according to His will He heareth us, and if we know that He hear us, whatsoever we ask, we know that we have the petitions that we desired of Him. Do you go to Him for heart purity? It is His will that you should receive, and if you ask in faith you can know that you have the petition that you desire of Him. Do you desire that Christ should dwell in your heart by faith? That is in accordance with His will. Ask and ye shall receive. Do you desire that the might of God's Spirit shall accompany your ministry? That is according to the will of God. Continue in the presence of your heavenly Father, quietly reminding Him that this is what you desire, and He will not fail to give you the exceeding abundantly above all you ask or think. He will fill you with rivers - the blessed rivers of the Spirit - and flowing from the midst of you they will be blessings to all that are around.

In the introduction to his second epistle Peter addresses "them that have obtained like precious faith with us." It is written, "They that trust in the Lord shall be as Mount Zion which cannot be removed." Have you this faith of divine origin springing up in your heart? It will make you steadfast and unmovable. This faith, this confidence, this trust in God, will have a transforming power; changing and transforming spirit, soul, and body, sanctifying the entire being.

"Faith comes by hearing, and hearing by the Word of God." It is God coming in by His Word and laying the solid foundation. Faith is like dynamite which bursts up the old life and nature by the power of God, and brings the almighty power of God into the life. This substance will diffuse through the whole being, bringing everything else into insignificance. The Word of God is formed within the temple. Jeremiah spoke of the Word as a "fire within." It is a power stronger than granite that is able to resist the mightiest pressure the devil can bring against it. Faith counts on God's coming forth to confound the enemy. Faith count son the display of God's might, when it is needful for Him to come forth in power.

In these eventful days we must not be content with a mere theory of faith, but must have this almighty and precious faith within us so that we may move from the ordinary into the extraordinary. We must expect Him to come forth in power through us for the deliverance of others. Peter spoke of it as "like precious faith." It is a like kind to that which Abraham had - the very faith of God. When Peter and John said to the lame man, Such as we have we give thee. In the name of Jesus Christ of Nazareth rise up and walk, there was a manifestation of the same faith that Abraham had. It is this like precious faith God wants us to have.

In the former days the prophets received the Holy Spirit in a certain measure, but the Holy Spirit was given to the Lord Jesus Christ without measure. Did not He give the Holy Spirit on the Day of Pentecost in this same measureless measure? That is His thought for you and me. Since I received the mighty Baptism in the Holy Spirit God has flooded my life with His power. From time to time there have been wonderful happenings - to Him be all the glory. Faith in God will bring the operation of the Spirit and we'll have the divine power flooding the human vessel and flowing out in blessing to others.

Faith is made in hard places when we are at wit's-end corner, and there seems no way out of our adversity. David said at one time, "The sorrows of death compassed made me afraid. The sorrows of hell compassed me about." He tells us, "In my distress I called upon the Lord, and cried unto my God: he heard my voice out of his temple . . . he bowed the heavens. . . and came down." Faith cries to God in the place of testing. It is in these places that God enlarges us and brings us forth into a large place, to prove Himself the God of deliverances, the One who is indeed our helper.

I remember in the year 1920 after a most distressing voyage I went straight from the ship on which I had been traveling, to a meeting. As I entered the building a man fell down across the doorway in a fit. The Spirit of the Lord was upon me and I commanded the demon to leave. Some years later I visited this same assembly, and I ventured to ask if anyone remembered the incident. A man stood up and I told him to come to the platform. He told me that on that day he had been delivered by the name of Jesus and had not had a fit since. We read in Acts 10:38 that "God hath anointed Jesus of Nazareth with the Holy Ghost and with power: who went about doing good, and healing all that were oppressed of the devil; for God was with him." God wants us to have this same anointing and same power. through the indwelling Christ and through a living faith. It was the Lord Himself who told us before He went away, "These signs shall follow them that believe. In my name they shall cast out demons . . . they shall lay hands on the sick and they shall recover." God is waiting to manifest His divine power through believers.

I remember a man coming to me suffering with cancer, who said he had been twelve years in pain. The power of the Lord was present to heal, and that night he came back to the meeting with all his sores dried up.

In this second epistle of Peter we further read, "According to his divine power hath given unto us all things that pertain unto life and godliness through the knowledge of him that hath called us to glory and virtue: whereby are given unto us exceeding great and precious promises :that by these ye might be partakers of the divine nature." Believe the record, His divine power has provided this life and godliness and virtue. Believe for the virtue of the Lord to be so manifested through your body that as men touch you they are healed. Believe for the current to go through you to others. It is amazing what can happen when some necessity arises when there is no time to pray, only to act. It is in such times of necessity that the Holy Ghost comes forth to act.

We must so live in God that the Spirit of God can operate through us. I remember being in one place where there were 6,000 people outside the building where we were preaching. Many of them were in chairs, waiting for hands to be laid on them and the prayer of faith to be offered. Oh for the virtue that flowed from Christ to touch the needy everywhere!

A woman said to Christ one time, "Blessed is the womb that bare thee, and the paps which thou hast sucked." But he answered, "Yea rather, blessed are they hath hear the word. of God, and keep it." It is through the hearing of the Word of God that faith comes, and faith brings the omnipotence of God to helpless souls and brings the virtue of Christ to the sick and to the needy. Do you remember how they asked the Lord, "What shall we do that we might work the works of God?" Jesus answered and said unto them, "This is the work of God that ye believe on him whom he hath sent." He further said, "The works that I do shall ye do also: and greater works than these shall ye do; because I go unto my Father." There is nothing impossible to faith.

When I was in Orebro 12 years ago I ministered to a girl who was twelve years' old, and blind. When I last went to Orebro they told me that she had had perfect sight from that day. The Lord Himself challenges us to believe Him when He says, "Have faith in God." "Verily, I say unto you, That whosoever shall say unto this mountain., Be thou removed, and be thou cast into the sea; and shall not doubt in his heart, but shall believe that those things which he saith shall come to pass; he shall have whatsoever he saith." Did you get that? "He shall have whatsoever he saith." When you speak in faith your desire is an accomplished thing. Our Lord further said, "Therefore I say unto you, What things soever ye desire, when ye pray, believe that ye receive them, and ye shall have them."

In one place a man said to me, "You helped a good many today, but you have not helped me." I said, "What is the trouble?' He said, "I cannot sleep, and I am losing my reason." I said to him, "Believe." And then I told him to go home and sleep, and I told him I would believe God. He went home and his wife said to him, "Well, did you see the preacher?" And he said, "He helped everyone but me." However, he fell asleep. His wife said, "I wonder if it is all right." Morning, noon, and night he was still asleep, but he woke bright and happy, rested and restored. What had brought about this restoration? Faith in God! "He shall have whatsoever he saith." Have you received this "like precious faith"? If so, deal bountifully with the oppressed. God has called us to loose the bands of wickedness. undo the heavy burden, let the oppressed go free, and break the yokes that the devil has put upon them. Pray in faith. Remember he that asketh receiveth. Ask and it shall be given you. Live for God. Keep clean and holy. Live under the unction of the Holy Spirit. Let the mind of Christ be yours so that you live in God's desires and plans. Glorify Him in the establishment of His blessing upon the people, and in seeing God's glory manifested in the midst. Amen.

The Power of Christ's Resurrection

That I may know him, and the power of his resurrection, and the fellowship of his sufferings, being made conformable unto his death...I count not myself to have apprehended: but this one thing I do, forgetting those things which are behind, and reaching forth unto those things which are before, I press toward the mark for the prize of the high calling of God in Christ Jesus. Philippians 3: 10,13-14

What a wonderful Word! This surely means to press on to be filled with all the fullness of God. If we leak out here we shall surely miss God, and shall fail in fulfilling the ministry He would give us.

PRESSING ON FOR FULLER POWER

The Lord would have us preach by life, and by deed, always abounding in service; living epistles, bringing forth to men the knowledge of God. If we went all the way with God, what would happen? What should we see if we would only seek to bring honor to the name of our God? Here we see Paul pressing in for this. There is no standing still. We must move on to a fuller power of the Spirit, never satisfied that we have apprehended all, but filled with the assurance that God will take us on to the goal we desire to reach, as we press on for the prize ahead.

Abraham came out from Ur of the Chaldees. We never get into a new place until we come out from the old one. There is a place where we leave the old life behind, and where the life in Christ fills us and we are filled with His glorious personality.

On the road to Damascus, Saul of Tarsus was apprehended by Christ. From the first he sent up a cry, "Lord, what wilt thou have me to do?" He desired always to do the will of God, but here he realized a place of closer intimacy, a place of fuller power, of deeper crucifixion. He sees a prize ahead and every fiber of his being is intent on securing that prize. Jesus Christ came to be the firstfruits; the firstfruits of a great harvest of like fruit, like unto Himself. How zealous is the farmer as he watches his crops and sees the first shoots and blades. They are the earnest of the great harvest that is coming. Paul here is longing that the Father's heart shall be satisfied, for in that first resurrection the Heavenly Husbandman will see a firstfruits harvest, firstfruits like unto Christ, sons of God made conformable to the only begotten Son of God.

You say, "I am in a needy place." It is in needy places that God delights to work. For three days the people that were with Christ were without food, and He asked Philip, "From whence shall we buy bread that these may eat?" That was a hard place for Philip, but not for Jesus, for He knew perfectly what He would do. The hard place is where He delights to show forth His miraculous power. And how fully was the need provided for. Bread enough and to spare!

THE PRESENCE OF THE RISEN CHRIST
Two troubled, baffled travelers are on the road to Emmaus. As they communed together and reasoned, Jesus Himself drew near, and He opened up the Word to them in such a way that they saw light in His light. Their eyes were holden that they could not recognize who it was talking with them. But, oh how their hearts burned within as He opened up the Scripture to them. And at the breaking of bread He was made known to them. Always seek to be found in the place where He manifests His presence and power.

The resurrected Christ appeared to Peter and a few more of them early one morning on the shore of the lake. He prepared a meal for the tired, tried disciples. This is just like Him. Count on His presence. Count on His power. Count on His provision. He is always there just where you need Him.

Have you received Him? Are you to be found "in Him"? Have you received His righteousness, which is by faith? Abraham got to this place, for God gave this righteousness to him because he believed, and as you believe God He puts His righteousness to your account. He will put His righteousness right within you. He will keep you in perfect peace as you stay your mind upon Him and trust in Him. He will bring you to a rest of faith, to a place of blessed assurance that all that happens is working for your eternal good.

Here is the widow's son on the road to burial. Jesus meets that unhappy procession. He has compassion on that poor woman who is taking her only son to the cemetery. His great heart had such compassion that death had no power - it could no longer hold its prey. Compassion is greater than suffering. Compassion is greater than death. O God, give us this compassion! In His infinite compassion Jesus stopped that funeral procession and cried to that widow's son, "Young man, I say unto thee, Arise." And he who was dead sat up, and Jesus delivered him to his mother.

CHANNELS FOR HIS POWER

Paul got a vision and revelation of the resurrection power of Christ, and so he was saying, "I will not stop until I have laid hold of what God has laid hold of me for." For what purpose has God laid hold of us? To be channels for His power. He wants to manifest the power of the Son of God through you and me. God helps us to manifest the faith of Christ, the compassion of Christ, the resurrection power of Christ.

One morning about eleven o'clock I saw a woman who was suffering with a tumor. She could not live through the day. A little blind girl led me to the bedside. Compassion broke me up and I wanted that woman to live for the child's sake. I said to the woman, "Do you want to live?" She could not speak. She just moved her finger. I anointed her with oil and said, "In the name of Jesus." There was a stillness of death that followed; and the pastor, looking at the woman, said to me, "She is gone."

When God pours in His compassion it has resurrection power in it. I carried that woman across the room, put her against a wardrobe, and held her there. I said, "In the name of Jesus, death, come out." And soon her body began to tremble like a leaf. "In Jesus' name, walk," I said. She did and went back to bed.

I told this story in the assembly. There was a doctor there and he said, "I'll prove that." He went to the woman and she told him it was perfectly true. She said, "I was in heaven, and I saw countless numbers all like Jesus. Then I heard a voice saying, 'Walk, in the name of Jesus.'"

There is power in the name of Jesus. Let us apprehend it, the power of His resurrection, the power of His compassion, the power of His love. Love will break the hardest thing - there is nothing it will not break.

What wilt Thou have Me to do?

An Address at The Monday Meeting, Corinthian Hall, Oakland, Cal. Reported by Miss Sadie Cody. October 1914

Read Acts 19. As soon as Paul saw the light from heaven above the brightness of the sun, he said, "Lord, what wilt thou have me to do?" (Acts 9:6). And as soon as he was willing to yield he was in a condition where God could meet his need; where God could display His power; where God could have the man. Oh, beloved, are you saying today, "What wilt thou have me to do?" The place of yieldedness is just where God wants us.

People are saying, "I want the baptism, I want healing, I would like to know of a certainly that I am a child of God," and I see nothing, absolutely nothing in the way except unyieldedness to the plan of God. The condition was met which Paul demanded, and instantly when he laid hands on them they were filled with the Spirit and spoke in other tongues and prophesied (Acts 19:6). The only thing needed was just to be in the condition where God could come in. The main thing today that God wants is obedience. When you begin yielding and yielding to God He has a plan for your life, and you come in to that wonderful place where all you have to do is to eat the fruits of Canaan. I am convinced that Paul must have been in divine order as well as those men, and Paul had a mission right away to the whole of Asia.

Brothers and sisters, it is the call of God that counts. Paul was in the call of God. Oh, I believe God wants to stir somebody's heart today to obedience; it may be for China or India or Africa, but the thing God is looking for is obedience.

"What wilt thou have me to do?" (Acts 9:6).

...God wrought special miracles by the hands of Paul: so that from his body were brought unto the sick handkerchiefs or aprons, and the diseases departed from them, and the evil spirits went out of them. Acts 19:11,12

If God can have His way today, the ministry of somebody will begin; it always begins as soon as you yield. Paul had been bringing many people to prison, but God brought Paul to such a place of yieldedness and brokenness that he cried out, "What wilt thou have me to do?" (Acts 9:6). Paul's choice was to be a bondservant for Jesus Christ. Beloved, are you willing that God shall have His way today? God said, "I will show him how great things he must suffer for my name's sake" (Acts 9:16). But Paul saw that these things were working out a far more exceeding weight of glory. You people who have come for a touch from God, are you willing to follow Him; will you obey Him?

When the prodigal son had returned and the father had killed the fatted calf and made a feast for him, the elder brother was angry and said, "...thou never gavest me a kid, that I might make merry with my friends," (Luke 15:29) but the father said to him, "...all that I have is thine" (v. 31). He could kill a fatted calf at any time. Beloved, all in the Father's house is ours, but it will come only through obedience. And when He can trust us, we will not come behind in anything.

"...God wrought special miracles by the hands of Paul" (Acts 19:11). Let us notice the handkerchiefs that went from his body; it means to say that when he touched and sent them forth, God wrought special miracles through them, and diseases departed from the sick, and evil spirits went out of them. Is it not lovely? I believe after we lay hands on these handkerchiefs and pray over them, that they should be handled very sacredly, and even as the one carries them they will bring life, if they are carried in faith to the suffering one. The very effect of it, if you only believed, would change your own body as you carried it.

A woman came to me one day and said, "My husband is such a trial to me; the first salary he gets he spends it in drink, and then he cannot do his work and comes home; I love him very much, what can be done?" I said, "If I were you I would take a handkerchief and would place it under his head when he went to sleep at night, and say nothing to him, but have a living faith." We anointed a handkerchief in the name of Jesus, and she put it under his head. Oh, beloved, there is a way to reach these wayward ones. The next morning on his way to work he called for a glass of beer; he lifted it to his lips, but he thought there was something wrong with it, and he put it down and went out. He went to another saloon, and another, and did the same thing. He came home sober. His wife was gladly surprised and he told her the story; how it had affected him. That was the turning point in his life; it meant not only giving up drink, but it meant his salvation.

God wants to change our faith today. He wants us to see it is not obtained by struggling and working and pining. "...the Father himself loveth you..." (John 16:27). "...Himself took our infirmities, and bare our sicknesses" (Matthew 8:17). "Come unto me, all ye that labor and are heavy laden, and I will give you rest" (Matthew 11:28).

Who is the man that will take the place of Paul, and yield and yield and yield, until God so possesses him in such a way that from his body virtue shall flow to the sick and suffering? It will have to be the virtue of Christ that flows. Don't think there is some magic virtue in the handkerchief or you will miss the virtue; it is the living faith in the man who lays the handkerchief on his body, and the power of God through that faith. Praise God, we may lay hold of this living faith today. "The blood has never lost its power." As we get in touch with Jesus, wonderful things will take place; and what else? We shall get nearer and nearer to Him.

There is another side to it. "...exorcists, took upon them to call over them which had evil spirits the name of the Lord Jesus, saying, We adjure you by Jesus whom Paul preacheth...and the evil spirit answered and said, Jesus I know, and Paul I know; but who are ye?" (Acts 19:13,15). I beseech you in the name of Jesus, especially those of you who are baptized, to awaken up to the fact that you have power if God is with you; but there must be a resemblance between you and Jesus. The evil spirit said, "...Jesus I know, and Paul I know; but who are ye?" (Acts 19:15). Paul had the resemblance.

You are not going to get it without having His presence; His presence changes you. You are not going to be able to get the results without the marks of the Lord Jesus. The man must have the divine power within himself; devils will take no notice of any power if they do not see the Christ. "Jesus I know, and Paul I know; but who are ye?" The difference between these men was they had not the marks of Christ, so the manifestation of the power of Christ was not seen.

You want power: don't take the wrong way. Don't take it as power because you speak in tongues, and if God has given you revelations along certain lines don't take that for the power; or if you have even laid hands on the sick and they have been healed, don't take that for the power. "The Spirit of the Lord is upon me..." (Luke 4:18); that alone is the power. Don't be deceived; there is a place to get where you know the Spirit is upon you, so you will be able to do the works which are wrought by this blessed Spirit of God in you, and the manifestation of His power shall be seen, and people will believe in the Lord.

What will make men believe the divine promises of God? Beloved, let me say to you today, God wants you to be ministering spirits, and it means to be clothed with another power. And this divine power, you know when it is there, and you know when it goes forth. The baptism of Jesus must bring us to have a single eye to the glory of God; everything else is wasted time and wasted energy. Beloved, we can reach it; it is a high mark but we can get to it. You ask how? "What wilt thou have me to do?" That is the plan. It means a perfect surrender to the call of God, and perfect obedience.

A dear young Russian came to England. He did not know the language, but learned it quickly and was very much used and blessed of God; and as the wonderful manifestations of the power of God were seen, they pressed upon him to know the secret of his power, but he felt it was so sacred between him and God he should not tell it, but they pressed him so much he finally said to them: "First God called me, and His presence was so precious, that I said to God at every call I would obey Him, and I yielded, and yielded, and yielded, until I realized that I was simply clothed with another power altogether, and I realized that God took me, tongue, thoughts and everything, and I was not myself but it was Christ working through me." How many of you today have known that God has called you over and over, and has put His hand upon you, but you have not yielded? How many of you have had the breathing of His power within you, calling you to prayer, and you have to confess you have failed?

I went to a house one afternoon where I had been called, and met a man at the door. He said, "My wife has not been out of bed for eight months; she is paralyzed. She has been looking so much for you to come, she is hoping God will raise her up." I went in and rebuked the devil's power. She said, "I know I am healed; if you go out I will get up." I left the house, and went away not hearing anything more about her. I went to a meeting that night, and a man jumped up and said he had something he wanted to say; he had to go to catch a train but wanted to talk first. He said, "I come to this city once a week, and I visit the sick all over the city. There is a woman I have been visiting and I was very much distressed about her; she was paralyzed and has lain on that bed many months, and when I went there today she was up doing her work." I tell this story because I want you to see Jesus.

We had a letter which came to our house to say that a young man was very ill. He had been to our Mission a few years before with a very bad foot; he had no shoe on, but a piece of leather fastened on the foot. God healed him that day. Three years after, something else came upon him. What it was I don't know, but his heart failed, and he was helpless; he could not rise or dress or do anything for himself, and in that condition he called his sister and told her to write and see if I would pray. My wife said to go, and she believed God would give me that life. I went, and when I got to this place I found the whole country was expecting me; they had said that when I came this man would be healed. I said to the woman when I arrived, "I have come." "Yes," she said, "but it is too late." "Is he alive?" I asked, "Yes, just alive," she said. I went in and put my hands upon him, and said, "Martin." He just breathed slightly, and whispered, "The doctor said if I move from this position I will never move again." I said, "Do you know the Scripture says, 'God is the strength of my heart, and my portion forever'?" (Psalm 73:26). He said, "Shall I get up?" I said, "No."

That day was spent in prayer and ministering the Word. I found a great state of unbelief in that house, but I saw Martin had faith to be healed. His sister was home from the asylum. God held me there to pray for that place. I said to the family, "Get Martin's clothes ready; I believe he is to be raised up." I felt the unbelief. I went to the chapel and had prayer with a number of people around there, and before noon they too believed Martin would be healed. When I returned I said, "Are his clothes ready?" They said, "No." I said, "Oh, will you hinder God's work in this house?" I went in to Martin's room all alone. I said, "I believe God will do a new thing today. I believe when I lay hands on you the glory of heaven will fill the place." I laid my hands on him in the name of the Father, Son, and Holy Ghost, and immediately the glory of the Lord filled the room, and I went headlong to the floor. I did not see what took place on the bed, or in the room, but this young man began to shout out, "Glory, glory!" and I heard him say, "for Thy glory, Lord," and that man stood before me perfectly healed. He went to the door and opened it and his father stood there. He said, "Father, the Lord has raised me up," and the father fell to the floor and cried for salvation. The young woman brought out of the asylum was perfectly healed at that moment by the power of God in that house.

God wants us to see that the power of God coming upon people has something more in it than we have yet known. The power to heal and to baptize is in this place, but you must say, "Lord, what wilt thou have me to do?" You say it is four months before the harvest. If you had the eyes of Jesus you would see that the harvest is already here. The devil will say you can't have faith; you tell him he is a liar. The Holy Ghost wants you for the purpose of manifesting Jesus through you. Oh, may you never be the same again! The Holy Spirit moving upon us will make us to be like Him, and we will truly say, "Lord, what wilt thou have me to do?"